A Woman's GUIDE TO UNDERSTANDING MEN

Dating Secrets Most Women Don't Know

A
Woman's
GUIDE TO UNDERSTANDING MEN

Dating Secrets Most Women Don't Know

Print ISBN: 978-1-7366755-1-9
Ebook ISBN: 978-1-7366755-0-2

KACM Media

FIRST EDITION

www.karennaalexander.com

Testimonials

"If you want to know what men really want and to mesmerize Mr. Right, buy this book now! *A Woman's Guide to Understanding Men* will take you into the inner workings of the male mind so you get fabulous results!"

Ellen Fein and Sherrie Schneider
authors of the *New York Times*
bestseller *The Rules*

"I used Karenna's tips to find my husband. They work like a charm. What I didn't realize until I started working with her is that my hard-driving personality was turning men off. She helped me understand men, and that made all the difference. She transformed my life."

Scarlet C. from Boston

"I had an amazing career but was clueless as to how to get a great boyfriend. Karenna gave me a crash course in understanding men, and I immediately realized what I was doing wrong. We worked on my look, my mindset, my actions, and my strategy, and I met a great guy in four months. We got engaged after nine months! Without her advice I would never have been able to get engaged to such a quality guy. There's more to getting a great guy and keeping him than many smart ladies today realize."

Michelle P. from Canada

"I got the best headshot for my online dating profile after consulting with Karenna. She has the best hair and beauty and clothes tips. My before and after online dating photos are like night and day. The number of emails I get from men has exploded. She really knows what she is doing."

Molly Z. from London

"I was a basket case when I first came to Karenna for coaching. I couldn't understand why relationship after relationship didn't work out. Karenna taught me so much, helping me understand men and why I needed to change my behavior around them. I was pushing men away by my intensity and in other ways. After several coaching sessions and taking her fun and incredibly fabulous 'Frumpy to Fabulous' course, I met a great guy, and my whole life turned around. I got the fairy tale boyfriend I always wanted: smart, cute, funny, and most importantly he treats me like

I'm the hottest woman on the planet. Looking back, I wish I was taught this in high school! I would have saved myself so much man pain."

Sara L. from Switzerland

"Karenna helped me get out there and date more after a really bad breakup. I was initially afraid to go online (I was so worried about people seeing me there). But she helped me be confident about getting out there, in every way, shape, or form, and I am dating more than any of my friends. Some of my friends look like models, yet they are envious of me because I have lots of great dates! Crazy, right?"

Samantha B. from Paris

Dedication

To my mother, Joan—beautiful, loving, and a visionary. She always believed I would write a book someday.

Notes

The names of the women and men interviewed for the book were changed, as were identifying details in their stories.

Also, this book is intended for women seeking a heterosexual relationship. As a straight woman who had many epiphanies about men and dating before I became a dating coach, I wanted to share what I learned to help other women. My specialty is working with straight women dating men. However, I work with LGBTQ+ clients who are helped by my coaching, especially when it comes to boundaries and confidence. If you're a member of the LGBTQ+ community and you're reading this book, that's great. If any aspect of the book resonates with you, feel free to take what you like and leave the rest.

Table of Contents

Introduction

An amazing, attractive man who treats you like gold is well within your grasp, but finding him may feel elusive. You're not alone — many smart, successful, beautiful women feel the same. Quite simply, they don't understand men.

If you want the fairy tale you've always dreamed about, you must learn to understand men and to respect the differences between men and women. I wrote *A Woman's Guide to Understanding Men* to teach you how men *really* think, not how you *wish* men think. *A Woman's Guide to Understanding Men* will help you as a smart, successful woman who is conquering the world in every area but your romantic life.

Rest assured, there's hope. I'm here to teach you strategies that will make dating and relationships easier, more efficient, and less stressful. My strategies will help you weed out Mr. Wrongs quickly and cause Mr. Right to fall hard.

Because most women don't understand men, they don't have the right game plan to weed out the wrong men. They don't have the strategies to find Mr. Right and have a healthy relationship. They don't know how to make or keep a man happy.

This book isn't intended for those looking for casual hookups or dating only to have fun. This book is for a woman looking for her Mr. Forever. You need to understand how a good man in love behaves — never making excuses or letting him off the hook. You also need to do your part in bringing out the best in a man. When you understand this, you won't settle for anything less again.

If you want a loving relationship with the man of your dreams, the best way to achieve that is to hold out for courtship. Yes, that's right: courtship. Courtship is the key to a successful modern-day relationship.

Proper courtship is a metaphorical slow dance that leads to a serious relationship or marriage. Courtship is the process of getting to know one another slowly over a period of many months. Courtship is slow and steady. It's also romantic and can be intense. With proper courtship, man pursues woman. He asks her out. He plans dates. He pays. He pushes the romance forward.

A man is the pursuer, and the woman is the receiver. While a woman lets the man lead, she isn't passive. She evaluates whether the man she's dating is right for her, never letting lust blind her during the courtship dance.

This book explores proper courtship and how good men who like you will respond to it. I explain why these courtship principles work so well for modern women who don't want to waste time as they search for Mr. Right.

Not only does courtship weed out time wasters extremely fast, it also gives a man a challenge and creates a spark that helps lay the foundation for a beautiful relationship. Men remember those first few months forever. If you put these principles in place early on, a man will treasure you throughout the dating process and beyond. It's something he'll remember 50 years later. He won't forget how lucky he was to get you and how good he felt inside while he was courting you.

Courtship helps you achieve a special brand of love,

where your man cherishes you. He's romantic, protective, and generous. He looks at you as if you're the most beautiful woman in the world. Unconditional love is the payoff.

In this day and age, courtship is a bold philosophy. But it works. It's not always easy to follow these strategies, but the rewards are priceless. If you want a high-quality relationship with a high-quality man, hold out for courtship.

The modern courtship strategies I write about in this book are critical. But first you need to grasp what men are *really* like. When a client is struggling to follow courtship principles, I find when I explain men's psyches, she has a lightbulb moment and realizes why courtship works.

When a man is in love with a woman, he responds to courtship. When a man is lukewarm, he isn't able to jump through all the courtship hoops and gets weeded out quickly. When you allow a man to court you, you'll find out fast if he's *the one* or if he's wasting your time.

If you have trouble receiving from men (whether it's letting him pay for dinner, accepting his love, or other ways) or if you don't respect the differences between men and women, a guy won't insist on courting you. When you won't allow a man to court you, he'll start treating you in a casual manner. And when he doesn't court you properly, he's likely treating you as an afterthought.

You may have heard about courtship principles before but dismissed them. Once you read this book and start to see how men are different in the dating arena, you'll know why courtship is necessary and will have more harmonious relationships with men. It comes down to the fact that men and women are different biologically, and men respond differently than women in relationships. Understanding these differences empowers you.

What you get when you follow these strategies are dreamy guys who are in it for the long haul. Your relationships flow. You have a spark with a gorgeous guy who likes you back.

Modern-day courtship is a beautiful thing because it frees you up to meet men who truly like you. It ends the despair and frustration over unrequited love or a love life that's been frustrating or painful for years. When you get how men think, you'll get off that hamster wheel and fall into the arms of an adoring man.

This book will teach you to get Mr. Right to fall hard for you and propose. Even if you aren't looking for marriage, the strategies in this book will give you boundaries and teach you how to date healthily so that men treat you well, whether you want to get married or simply have a long-term relationship.

If your confidence has taken a hit and you feel like your best days are behind you, fret not. No matter your age or what you've been through emotionally or physically, you can be a man's dream girl.

If you're not getting first, second, or third dates, or if you're falling for the wrong guys, getting dumped, or in a lackluster unhealthy relationship, keep reading.

My wisdom is based on years of observing men's actions, both in my personal and professional life. Because of my experience as a dating expert who has been in the trenches, I know what works. I know how it really is out there.

I'm also a trained observer with a master's degree from Columbia University's Graduate School of Journalism. I'm a former matchmaker, certified by the Matchmaking Institute in New York City, and I worked with many men in that capacity.

I interviewed and observed hundreds of men for this book and watched their actions, including how they followed through on their words.

All this to say, I know what men are thinking, even better than they do. Men don't think rationally when attracted to a woman.

I didn't always have this knowledge, but had an epiphany when I read a book called *The Rules: Time-tested Secrets for Capturing the Heart of Mr. Right,* by Ellen Fein and Sherrie Schneider (1995). The book explains the importance of courtship principles, like letting a man lead and letting him pay.

The authors of *The Rules* helped me immensely in my own life, and I used the knowledge they so generously shared with me to help other women. I became a certified Rules dating coach to help other women transform their lives as well. What I noticed over and over again is that the more I help women understand men and how they think and how they behave when they are in love, the more they understand why this philosophy — one which, on the surface, seems so retro — really works for modern women.

I Get The Controversy

Many smart, successful women today think courtship is beneath them. When I first read an article about *The Rules,* I thought courtship was silly. I remember telling a male co-worker about the article, and when he said it was smart, I was stunned.

I got into a debate with him, and I started to think he was a jerk. (Sorry, Bob!) I thought by agreeing with the philosophy, he saw women as second-class citizens and wanted women to be subservient to men.

The Rules philosophy isn't creating the unfairness. It's simply showing the reality and how to adapt to it.

Modern women are conflicted over this because women are equal to men and go after what they want in all areas of their lives. Women go after stunning apartments, amazing jobs, incredible adventures, and exotic trips. Women want to pull out all the stops and win over the man they want, too.

But unfortunately, it doesn't work to go after the guy you want. Letting a man lead is an essential aspect of courtship. If this is tough for you to accept, it's important to realize that when you're dating a guy who makes the first move, you're more in control than you realize. You know he's into you since he chose you. If a guy isn't stepping up by moving a relationship forward, you have your answer. It's freeing and a much less stressful way to date.

You Deserve The Fairy Tale

Courtship may be retro, but it works in today's modern age of dating. While some people may criticize modern-day women for wanting to be properly courted, the women I coach into successful relationships don't care that this advice isn't considered politically correct. My clients know these strategies are smart and healthy. These women are getting the beautiful brand of love they want with great guys. And they're making their men happy. The men are weak in the knees over these women because they're special and rare, and men treat them that way.

I want you to become just as giddy as my clients are about their love lives. I want you to have all the secrets.

Courtship is not only better for you — it's also ideal for the man you're dating. A man wants to *feel* something for the hot girl he's dating. He wants the thrill of getting her. He doesn't want the pursuit to be over so quickly. Pursuing a woman is an exciting challenge, and it gives him much-needed space.

If you're not allowing the man you're with to court you, you're being robbed — and shortchanging him, too. Once you've been courted properly, you'll realize you can't go back.

My client Wren, age 36, from Los Angeles, met her sexy boyfriend Ted, 42, through mutual friends, and he liked her right away. She liked him, too. It would have been easy to get swept up in a fast and furious romance. Because she'd learned to understand men and proper courtship, she paced the relationship and only saw him once a week in the early stages. He begged to see her more, but she knew it would be better to go slow — giving too much too soon to a man, even one who was excited about her, would work against her.

Because Wren prioritized courtship and had strong boundaries, Ted introduced her to his family and friends quickly and planned special occasions in advance. He bought her romantic gifts, and the most exciting present of all was the beautiful Tiffany's engagement ring he picked. He's been involved in all the wedding planning. "The best part is that he's loving and caring all the time. I am so happy," Wren said.

It's thrilling when relationships progress like clockwork — the Saturday night dates, the flowers, cute texts during the week, and commitment from a man who loves you deeply. This kind of man is attentive and is there for you when you're sick. He speaks about how he's never met anyone like you before. He's there for you with romantic presents on Valentine's Day and your birthday. He's there for your children. He uses "love" in conversation. This man wants to commit because you give him space. You're the dream girl he has waited for his whole life.

You understand men, and that's a sexy thing to a guy.

Women Have No Idea How Men Are Wired

The fact that men and women are wired differently might not seem like such a newsflash. But I can tell you from my experience as a dating coach, matchmaker, and from my personal life that many women have no idea how men think and why they behave as they do.

Whether these women are young, old, married, single, divorced, widowed, celebs, non-celebrities, live in the northern hemisphere or the southern hemisphere, it doesn't matter. There's a gap in their understanding of men, and this is where significant problems begin.

I've noticed the aggressive tendencies that have gotten women far in their careers have hurt them romantically. But it's not necessarily because men are intimidated by their success. A woman's success may intimidate some men, sure. But other times the problem is how a woman shows up in a relationship.

The courtship strategies I outline help you date with boundaries, which leads to confidence, and that makes you much sexier to men.

In this book, I'll also teach you not to waste time waiting for the ambivalent guy to fall for you.

This Book Will Be Your Best Friend

I've split the book into four key sections, each filled with scripts (check out the *Dream Girl Dialogue* sections at the end of every chapter) and strategies to guide you through the process of finding Mr. Right.

In Section One, *Weeding Out Time Wasters,* I teach you how a man in love behaves. You'll learn to efficiently and confidently eliminate the Mr. Wrongs. These weeding out strategies not only explain how to save precious time, but also cause Mr. Right to cherish you even more.

In Section Two, *Communication,* I explain the type of communication men *really* want. I tell you how to communicate with men so that they respect and adore you.

Section Three is about *Looks, Attitude, and Confidence.* In this section, I explain the role appearance plays in dating, and I tell you what men are looking for. There's a *lot* you can do in this area, even if you feel like your appearance has taken a hit. And while looks are important, you'll lose a man fast if you have a bad attitude and no self respect. If your attitude needs adjusting and your self esteem is in the dumps, you'll learn to turn things around.

Section Four contains more tips on *Getting to the Next Level.* This section discusses how long to date before making sure a man seals the deal, and it explains how to give a man a gentle push if he's not broaching a commitment. And I give you tips on what to do if one of you wants to end the relationship.

Spiritual Gym

The dating philosophy I write about will give you a high-quality relationship with a high-quality man. But for this to happen you need to be, or at least work toward becoming, a high-quality person yourself. You will notice that I reference a term *spiritual gym* throughout the book.

By spiritual gym, I mean a place where you go to work on the aspects of your personality that might be working against you while dating. If you're committed to following the dating philosophy I write about, you'll likely need to work on improving your mindset. Whether you feel like you're a tempestuous basket case or an evolved woman, there will be times that you will likely struggle to be your higher self.

The spiritual gym is a place to go to develop your inner game. Most people aren't born with all the tools to keep themselves content, confident, happy, and free from worry. Just like you need to work out your body to be in great shape, you need to keep your mindset healthy as well. This is why personal development is important.

Even the best of us can struggle. But being your lower self will work against you while dating. For example, you may want to nag the man you're dating because he doesn't work hard enough. Or you may have a perfectly amazing relationship but start sabotaging it by thinking the grass is greener on the other side. Or you might make a minor annoyance into a bigger problem than it really is and launch into an angry tirade against your boyfriend. These are the times you should go to the spiritual gym.

Not only will these tactics in the book help you become a better and healthier dater—you'll eventually become a healthier and more appealing serious girlfriend or wife.

The Right Way To Be Aggressive

This book isn't about being passive or a doormat. When you adhere to modern courtship principles, you have to wait for the right man to make the first move and subsequent moves. But you'll need to be proactive, taking action to meet relationship-minded men and initiating other important steps that I write about in this book. You should aggressively get out there to meet men, whether it be online, at social events, through friends, or any other way you can think of.

Besides taking aggressive social actions, you must take amazing care of yourself. You should work on both your inner game (your attitude, confidence, and more) and your outer game (appearance). You'll need to respect and enforce courtship, and you'll need to understand men and respect the romantic differences between men and women.

A Woman's Guide to Understanding Men explains how to do all of this and more. It only takes one guy, and the universe is abundant. He's out there!

SECTION ONE

Weeding Out

TIME WASTERS

CHAPTER 1

Mr. Right Does the Drive

A Man Will Drive for His Dream Girl– He Won't Insist You Meet Him Halfway

Don't date a man unless he's willing to drive to your area for dates.

A man who likes you will drive to you. When you understand this, you can easily weed out—in a heartbeat—players, unavailable men, and men who are lazy or lukewarm about you. When you allow a guy to court you by meeting you on your turf, you save precious time. Also, when a man does the drive, it allows him to work for you, which is a crucial part of courtship. He'll appreciate you much more if you aren't so easy to get.

Many women don't get this concept. Some don't have faith that a guy will do the drive, so they end up putting themselves in the driver's seat—literally and figuratively. They offer to drive, take Uber, or grab public transportation to his house or the city where he lives, or they meet him halfway. But when a guy *feels* something special for a woman, he'll make the effort to come to her area for a date.

Don't feel guilty about asking a man to make an effort. Women get dolled up for dates in high heels, makeup, and tight skirts. It's gentlemanly for a man to come to you so that you don't have to drive or take the subway when you're all dressed up. Men are willing to drive for hours to meet friends at hockey games, casinos, concerts, and other places where they can relax with friends. You're not asking for too much here.

If you think you need to drive to a man to get him, you may not have confidence that he likes you enough to drive to you. You may have difficulty receiving from men or from people in general. You may not feel worthy of true love. You also may not understand how a good man behaves when he's into you.

A good man who is attracted to you and sees a future with you will drive to your area to pick you up, then drive back to his area for a dinner date; then he'll drop you off at your house and drive all the way back home. I've seen this happen time and time again, even when the man lives more than an hour away. Men know how to court women if women allow the courting process to happen.

I've seen the opposite happen, too. Some men will ask women to do the drive. Often these guys are time wasters. Sometimes a man makes the offer more tempting by offering to pay for an Uber or limo. This can be hard to resist, especially if he's cute and plans an amazing date. But even this type of overture isn't gentlemanly. A guy should drive to you or take Uber or a limo himself in the initial stages of dating. It sets up the courtship that's so necessary to have the relationship of your dreams. The guys who won't drive to you, who insist you drive to them or meet halfway, are treating you way too casually.

A good guy who likes you may try to meet you in

between your respective houses or may ask you to drive to him at some point. Some men are spoiled and used to women driving to them, while others are confused about dating etiquette and expectations and may not know the proper way to court a woman. Don't get mad at a guy who tries to get you to drive to him or meet you halfway. Don't angrily tell him he must drive to you. Don't show you're frustrated, even if you are. Nicely stand your ground. If he's a good man who likes you, he'll drive to you.

It's chivalrous for a man to pick you up at your apartment or house for your date. An exception to picking you up at your house is in the beginning, especially if it's an online or blind date. Early on, for safety reasons, it's best if you meet a man at a public venue. Just make sure the venue is convenient for you. When you feel comfortable enough with a man to let him know where you live, have him pick you up at your home.

Traffic Won't Stop Mr. Right

Warren, 45, is a recently divorced father of three who lives in a suburb of Chicago. He said he wouldn't drive to meet a woman in the city of Chicago because of the heavy traffic he'd encounter.

"Traffic is a dealbreaker. No way," Warren said. "She has to live within a 20-mile radius."

Then I asked him, "What if it were Shakira? Would you drive for her?" (She's his celebrity crush.) "Of course

I would," he replied. Hold out for the guy who sees you as his crush.

There are times a man will drive but will be angry about it. This happened to my client, Ingrid, 44, from Canada, who met a man from the dating app Hinge. He lived about 45 miles from her, and after he walked into the restaurant late, he started complaining about how, due to traffic, it took him an hour and a half to get to her town. He then asked her a few questions but acted irritated and bored. She'd been working with me long enough to know Mr. Right wouldn't behave like this. She ended the date quickly.

Luckily, her next date, from Match was a few weeks later, with a guy who drove almost an hour to meet her. Throughout their courtship, he drove in traffic, rain, and bad thunderstorms. He never missed a Saturday night date, and they got engaged almost one year to the day they met. She still remembers that awful Hinge date because it was the last bad date before she met Mr. Right. "He was the last frog before I met my prince," Ingrid said.

Realize, too, that a man will fly to another continent for his dream girl. I had a heartwarming conversation recently with an acquaintance, Bo, 37, from Miami. She was showing me a ruby bracelet, a birthday gift from her husband. I asked her how they met—one of my favorite questions on the planet! She said her now husband had been living in Greece, but they had Facebook friends in common, and he saw her profile as a "friend suggestion." He thought she was beautiful and reached out to their mutual friends to get her contact information. He met her after flying to Miami, where they had a meal. The rest is history. A guy who likes you enough will fly to another continent to meet you.

Be Wary Of Complainers

Ingrid weeded out a major complainer quickly. But sometimes a man won't complain right away, as Ingrid's Hinge date did. This is a sad fact of dating. A relationship can start great, and then after a month of driving to you and doing all the right things, a man realizes he doesn't want to make the effort any longer. Or maybe he knew it all along but was dating you so he could sleep with you or show you off as a trophy or have someone to take to events. This is awful, but some men do this. Some guys like the chase, but they never have any intention of a serious relationship. He may have enjoyed being with you, but the effort to see you becomes too much, and he decides you're not worth the work.

This is certainly a frustrating situation, and it can hurt, but when a relationship ends because a man won't drive to you, see it as a good thing. Instead of cursing the darkness, light a candle and thank the universe for weeding him out sooner rather than later. The signs are clear, and if you're smart, you'll heed them. Free up space so Mr. Right can find you. It's better to pull that bandage off fast than to endure the pain of unrequited love over a longer period.

This is why multi-dating (dating several men at the same time), even while you like one man a lot, is key. (See Chapter 8.)

Oldest Trick In The Book

Don't be impressed when a guy asks you to drive to his house so he can cook for you or if he asks to cook at your house. Or if he picks you up for your fourth date, for example, and drives to his area for a "surprise" and he pulls up to his house, saying he's going to cook you dinner.

His aim is to sleep with you, and if you aren't ready, you'll be in a difficult position. It's best to keep dates in the first three months (longer than three months is better) outside his or your home. It's a lazy way to court a woman in the initial stages. It's casual, and you don't want the relationship to get casual too quickly. Wait until you know what he's made of—what the relationship is made of—before you drive to his house and let him cook a meal for you.

Many women fall for this type of offer, thinking it's special. "He's cooking for me. How romantic. He's working for it." They get dressed up in beautiful makeup, clothes, and high heels and drive to his house. They serve themselves up to him on a silver platter by sleeping with him. This is when the romantic tension can start to fizzle.

A guy who asks to cook you dinner or who tries to spend a lot of time at your respective houses isn't necessarily a bad guy who's only in it for sex. He may see a future with you. Even nice guys push things along. They like you, so of course they want to have sex with you. But when you acquiesce to the "Let me make you dinner" offer too quickly, you kill the chase.

This doesn't mean you never let a guy in your house during the beginning stages of courtship. If a guy drives to your house bearing roses before your date, you can let him inside while you quickly put the flowers in a vase. After several consistent Saturday night dates, if you feel comfortable letting him inside after the date for a short bit, it's okay to do so if he asks to come in. Make sure you don't let things go too far sexually too quickly, though. If you're the type of person who struggles with self-control, it's best to not let him inside until you're ready to sleep with him. (See Chapter 2.)

Realize that this doesn't mean you never drive to a man you're dating. But for the most part, during courtship he should drive to you. This is an amazing weeding out tool. If he's committed to you, with serious talk of a future and a ring is imminent, you can drive and stay at his place on occasion.

Even before he talks about a serious future, there may be a special occasion that occurs when you can drive to his area, if things are going well in the relationship and he's doing all the right things. But these are exceptions.

This point raises the question of where to spend Saturday and other date nights when you start sleeping with a man. When you start sleeping together, it's better if the man stays over at your place. You should be comfortable; when you're in your home and in your surroundings, you're more at ease. However, there are reasons why this isn't always possible. For example, you may live with a relative or rent a room in someone's house, in which case there's no other option but to sleep at his house.

Also, you can eventually have a dinner date at your house or his house, but that's more for down the line when you're more confident about where things are going. Even then, be careful with home dates, because they can cause a relationship to get stale fast. During courtship, home dates should be the exception.

One of my clients, Mallory, 46, from Ohio, had her first home date with her fiancé, Ethan, 46, after they got engaged. In her case it was okay to accept a home date one Thursday night when Ethan asked if she could come for dinner and stay over. That night they were busy planning their wedding, and in the morning they had to get up early to visit Ethan's grandmother, who Ethan wanted to take for breakfast so she could get to know Mallory better. They were nearly married, and at this point Mallory knew he was a good guy who was seriously invested in the relationship.

The Bottom Line

In the initial stages of dating you must have dates on your turf. If a man objects, he's not your Mr. Right. When you allow a man to work to get you, he falls harder. You become a challenge and a thrill. A man who feels a spark for you responds to courtship, and driving to a woman is one of the biggies.

A man in it for the long haul will do the drive. He's worth waiting for.

Dream $\mathcal{Girl}$ Dialogue

Here's how to reply to a man who tries to get you to drive to his area for a date, and also how to respond to a man who tries to cook for you early in the dating process.

Say you live in Meaux, a town about 35 miles from Paris, and a guy you met online from Paris asks to meet you in downtown Paris. Tell him, **"Meaux works better for me,"** **"It would be better if you met me in Meaux,"** or **"Oh, sorry, I can't get there."**

When a guy you've met online—but never met in person—starts quibbling about how you should meet him at a place that's "in the middle" or convenient for him and not you, cut your losses and say or text, **"This isn't going to work out."** My client Stella, 37, from Portugal used that line on a man who insisted she meet him at a restaurant that was "sort of in the middle." He told her he would be doing most of the driving—because he was driving 41 minutes, and she was driving 24 minutes. When a guy's a bean counter like this before you've even met him, there will be more of the same down the line. This type of man likely doesn't respect or get courtship. (He also asked her dress size.)

If you've been dating a man who has been consistently

picking you up at your house, but after three months asks you to drive to his area, simply say, **"It would be better if you picked me up."** If he's a good guy who is into you, he'll come to you. As I said, some guys are spoiled by women who drive to them, and some don't understand courtship. This is why I say to give the guy a chance with the above dialogue. Say it nicely and not accusingly. If he refuses to drive to you, move on. You have better things to do.

If a guy decides in the initial stages of dating that he wants to cook dinner for you at his house or your house, nicely say, **"I'd prefer to go out."** A nice guy will get the message that you aren't ready to have home dates. You don't need to go anywhere fancy—that's not the point. The point is that the date should be outside his or your home.

A motivated man who sees you as his dream girl figures out fast what he needs to do to see you.

CHAPTER 2

Men Don't Want Casual Sex

It's More Exciting for a Man if You Don't Sleep with Him Right Away

Instead of hooking up, hold off.

When you like a man, make sure you wait to have sex with him. When you hold off, you end up weeding out men who are only dating you for sex. Just like other weeding out strategies in this book, waiting for sex shows you how a man feels about you. A good man who is interested in you won't drop you because you won't have sex with him right away.

Also realize that while sex will make you feel closer to a man emotionally, it won't have the same effect on him. When you sleep with a man too quickly, the challenge is over for him and a relationship can lose its passion quicker. You won't get the brand of love you deserve. If he's the right man for you, holding off until you're ready will actually cause him to feel closer to you.

Sex is a completely different experience for women than for men. Women get much more emotionally attached, and it's not in your best interest emotionally to have sex too soon, especially when you like a guy. Once you've slept with a man you like, it's harder to remain at an even emotional keel, pace a relationship, and keep the chase going. It's harder to think with a clear head and assess his character. If you hold off until you're fairly sure how he feels, you'll be more in control, which is better for you, better for him, and better for the relationship. Men, on the other hand, don't get as attached emotionally through sex.

A woman loses the power she has with a guy by sleeping with him too soon. If you sleep with a man—even one who seems crazy about you—before he gets a chance to fall for you and become emotionally invested, you risk him getting restless and possibly moving on to someone else. If he sleeps with you without getting to know or care for you, he may be more likely to move on to the next woman. If he falls for you hard—inside and outside—before you sleep together, he's more likely to stick around.

The right man will appreciate that you're holding back, even if he won't admit it. When you wait to have sex with a man, that elusive spark lasts longer, and you end up having a more romantic courtship. If a man breaks up with you before you sleep with him, he's done you a favor because you know sooner rather than later that he's not your guy, and you can move on in search of Mr. Right. You won't waste precious time.

The guys dating you to get lucky, the ones who aren't sure you're quite that special, those with no intention of a long-term relationship, may badger and guilt trip you into sleeping with them. Steer clear.

The man who feels something special for you is glad for the challenge and the excitement, the buildup to when you consummate your relationship. A man reading this might roll his eyes, saying, "Are you crazy?" But this is a gift you're giving a man and yourself. A relationship is much healthier and more exciting when you wait.

When a man is forced to wait, it's all he can think about. He says things like, "I want to make love to you so badly." He's plotting and planning ways to impress you.

I've seen again and again in my coaching practice how having sex too soon can cause problems for a healthy relationship. My clients who waited for several months are in amazing relationships. Their men can't believe their luck. It's a pure kind of love that's so rare in this day and age. These manly men turn sentimental over their paramour. In part, it's because the women delayed sex.

Relationships can and do last when women sleep with men early on, but the excitement gets cut short, and so does the courtship that's so important to lay a foundation for how he treats you in the future. You want to be with a man who doesn't take you for granted—and this can happen when a woman sleeps with a man too soon. You both deserve a beautiful courtship. Don't rush it. You can never get this fun and special period back.

How Long Should You Wait?

Wait at least three months. This is a general guideline. A lot depends on your situation. You may need to wait even longer. If you're dating the way I advocate in this book and you're only seeing a man once a week, in three months you will have gone on 12 or so dates. (See Chapter 6.) If you're following the courtship strategies in *A Woman's Guide to Understanding Men* and you make it to 12 dates with a man, there's a good chance he's a serious contender. This is important to know before you sleep with a man. You don't want to be another notch in a man's belt.

You may hear men joke that they won't date a woman if she doesn't sleep with him by the third date. But don't always listen to what men say. (More on this in Chapter 7.) In reality, when a man is with a special woman who he has a strong attraction and connection with, he'll wait. He may get grumpy, but he'll wait. And if he won't, he didn't really want you anyway.

Men's Thoughts On Casual Sex

A male friend of mine, Russ, 45, said that waiting can be more exciting because of the anticipation. He added, however, that even though the anticipation is exciting, he's not going to put the brakes on the sexual aspect of a relationship. "We're always ready to go," he said about men. You have to be the one to slow it down.

Geoff, 47, from Chicago, said all sorts of things swirl through his mind if a woman sleeps with him too soon. "First I think she must be really desperate. I know she may not be at all, but my thoughts go there." Then he said, "I start to think, 'Wow she must really like me.'" He also said he wants to pull back because he craves space, and he wonders if she's sleeping with everyone right away. "It's a double standard, but I can't help it. It's where my mind goes."

The Bottom Line

Hold back from sleeping with a man until you get a good feeling about him and where the relationship is going. When you wait at least three months, you weed out men only looking for sex. Delaying sex also allows you to have a more romantic and special courtship. It helps you stay in emotional control. It's better for you and the guy when you wait.

Who doesn't want a relationship filled with spark, anticipation, and excitement? The type where you pinch yourself because you feel like you're a character in a romantic love story?

Dream *Girl* Dialogue

When a man is trying to have sex with you before you want to, all you need to say is, **"I'm not ready."**

If he complains that physical intimacy isn't progressing fast enough, say, **"I'd like to go slow."**

Don't give a long explanation of how your ex-boyfriend hurt you and how you're trying to be careful this time. It makes you sound damaged. It's also none of his business. It shows you care a lot, and early on you don't want a man to know how much you care or else the chase and the mystery will be over.

If you're waiting until marriage to have sex—some women are—there'll be a point when he'll be pushing for sex. Once you start realizing he's a serious contender, it's only fair to let him know you don't want to be a tease. Say, **"It will be a while before I'm ready. I'm waiting."** He'll figure out that you're the type—whether it's for religious or other reasons—who is waiting until marriage to have sex. Don't say, "When we're married, I can sleep with you." When you bring up the word "marriage," you become the aggressor, pushing the relationship forward.

CHAPTER 3

A Man in Love Wants to Feed You

A Serious Contender Won't Go Dutch

Don't date a man who doesn't pick up the tab.

When you understand men, you'll notice that a good guy who's interested in you romantically will pay for dinner and the rest of the date. Or if your first date is for coffee or drinks, he'll pay for that. He wants to provide for you, protect you, and win you over.

When a man doesn't pay, you'll weed out someone who isn't that interested or who may not know how to treat a woman right. This type of man may be looking for a casual relationship and won't give you the courtship you deserve.

When a woman pays for or splits the tab on dates, the relationship sometimes does continue, lasting for months or years. But often it's problematic for the woman (and the man). If it leads to marriage, it may be more of a practical marriage rather than a romantic loving one. The reason I say it's problematic for the relationship is because it ends up going against courtship, which gives you a special brand of love and romance. When a woman splits the bill or pays for the tab, she's not allowing herself to be courted or treasured by a man. She's taking on the masculine pursuer role and when a woman does that, a man doesn't try as hard to impress her during courtship. She's less of a challenge, and the spark will dim.

Remember, the first few months of dating are crucial to laying a foundation for the entire relationship. A man will remember that period forever. When he's courting you by paying for you and following other courtship principles, he feels that essential spark, which is something he will never forget.

A tricky scenario comes up when a woman asks a man out (which by now, you've probably figured out is something I don't advocate). When a woman does this, the question of who pays gets confusing. Some men who are asked out by women offer to pay because they know it's a gentlemanly gesture. However, other times when a woman asks a man out, he'll want to go Dutch or will want the woman to pay, and I can't blame him. These men may never have wanted to be on the date in the first place. They didn't make the date happen, so they don't feel the desire to pay for the meal.

If a man who asks you out wants you to split the bill with him, split it, but never see him again. The reason I say to split the bill if he asks you to do so is because there's no need to be a drama queen and make a scene at a restaurant. Pay, gracefully exit, and never go out with him again. He's not your Mr. Right.

The places a man picks don't have to be ultra luxurious. And you shouldn't order the highest-priced item on the menu, either. Don't take advantage by ordering a costly bottle of champagne and the most expensive entree, plus a dessert and high-end after-dinner drinks. It's not right to take advantage of men for food, money, or perks.

Never Do "The Reach"

Sometimes a woman offers to pay, wanting to be polite. She reaches for the bill with no intention of paying for it. Don't do this. Besides being tacky and fake, it throws off the balance in a dating scenario.

Some guys will wonder if you're interested in them and get offended. Some men may feel like they don't need to court you any longer, and when they start thinking that, the relationship will get casual and stay that way. You won't get the romance you want or the courtship you deserve. A man won't treat you as his dream girl. He'll treat you like one of the guys or a co-worker.

You want your date to see you as special—that you're used to men wooing you. You're so used to men paying for you, you'd never think to offer. If this isn't true, you should act as if it's true, because it should be your reality.

Many women offer to pay but then get angry when their date acquiesces. Amanda, 39, a client from the UK, told me about a guy she was dating. After she insisted on paying, he agreed to let her split the check. She said she only offered out of politeness, not because she genuinely wanted to pay. She was annoyed at her date when he agreed. She refused to date him again. She wanted him to step up to the plate and pursue her, yet she wasn't making it easy. When you throw a wrench in the courting process, you can't necessarily blame a man when he doesn't properly court you. The solution is simple: Don't offer to pay for dinner or any other part of the date, like movies or shows. And if you offer and he acquiesces, don't get angry at him. You contributed to this.

Chivalry Isn't Dead

Some people—men and women—argue that it's unfair for men to pay all the time on dates. Some women have trouble with this concept for a lot of reasons. Some think they're being mean if they don't chip in. Some women want to pay because they want a man to respect them for their independence. They want the guy to see them as a strong woman who can take care of herself. They want the man to know they aren't a gold digger. Some women may be concerned about his financial state. I have even heard women say, "Guys want to be courted, too. You need to show him you care."

However, you need to realize that a good guy who is into you doesn't see it that way. Even if you make more money than he does, he'll want to pay. He knows he wants you in his life long-term, and his biological instincts will kick in and he'll want to show you he can take care of you. He's the type of guy who, when he sees that you're cold, gives you his jacket. When he drops you off after a date, he doesn't bolt before you've gotten inside your home.

Many women I work with are independent and can afford their own dinners, and they feel uncomfortable letting a man pay. But this is an important filtering tool, and it's a key part of courtship. It's important for women to get comfortable receiving.

It's chivalrous for a man to pay, and I don't believe chivalry is dead.

The Bottom Line

When you're with a man you like who asked you out, let him take care of the bill. When the check comes, there's no need to look at it or acknowledge the check in any way. Continue the conversation or finish your dessert. Wait for him to pick it up and pay. If he asks you to split or pay for dinner or any part of the date, pay for your part but don't see him again.

Don't throw a wrench in the courtship process by offering to pay. A man who feels a spark for you will pay on dates. If you're looking for a man who is all in, one who is going to be in it for the long haul, you need to wait for the one who pays on dates.

Dream *Girl* Dialogue

How should you thank a man who pays for your dinner? All you need to say is, **"Thanks,"** to your date as you're leaving the table or the restaurant or as the date's ending.

Don't be overly effusive. It's just dinner. He's getting a lot out of the date as well. He's spending time with a beautiful woman and likely plotting and planning how to impress you so he can sleep with you.

Also, when you're overly excited when thanking a man for dinner, you'll make him uncomfortable. He may wonder if this is the first time a man ever took you out for dinner. When he starts thinking that, you start losing your dream girl quality.

If you forget to thank a man at dinner, don't bother texting him afterward. Most men who are into you won't notice. They're so busy trying to impress you and plan that second date, they aren't holding a grudge.

If a guy notices that you didn't thank him and uses it as an excuse to lob criticism your way, then he has a bad attitude or is spiteful, angry, or petty. If this happens, it doesn't mean you're on the wrong track; it just means you had a date with Mr. Wrong. If a man tries to make you feel bad for wanting to be courted, he's not Mr. Right. Don't let a guy get you off course or make you think you're on the wrong path. Stay focused and keep on going.

This isn't the only scenario in dating where a man might be mean to you. It will happen in many dating situations when you try to enforce boundaries and when you hold out for a man who will court you. Again, this doesn't mean you're doing anything wrong. It means the guy isn't Mr. Right. Don't let any of this get you down. Don't waste energy arguing with the man. Just move on. Focus on your fabulous goals and keep your eye on the prize.

CHAPTER 4

Dreams are Made of Saturday Nights

If You're His Dream Girl, He'll Save the Best Night for You

When you like a man, only see him on Saturday nights.

Only going on dates on Saturday nights in the initial stages of dating is a great way to pace a relationship. Pacing is part of the courtship process that's so essential to having a romantic relationship. It also helps you figure out who is serious about you, because typically only men who really like you will consistently ask you out every Saturday night.

When you only see a man on Saturday night, he has all week to dream about you in anticipation of your date. Saturday date night becomes special.

Many women don't understand the importance of Saturday night dates. When a guy isn't with you on Saturday night, he could be with someone else or out hoping to meet someone else. Or he's with the guys, possibly on the prowl.

But here's one thing to keep in mind: just like some women don't understand the importance of Saturday night, sometimes men don't always know it either. Some men may have hung out with women all their dating lives yet may not understand courtship. They may have had girlfriends who were okay with them hanging out with the guys on Saturday night, so they aren't sure of its importance. Saturday may not have been treated by other women like the special day it is.

Because of this, there will be times when a man who is interested in you won't ask you out for Saturday nights but will ask for other nights. What you need to do in those cases is turn him down for every night except for Saturday. If he's perpetually not available on Saturday nights, then you have your answer—something else is going on that night, and it's not with you. Or he's not that serious about figuring out what he needs to do to date you.

If he's skipping Saturday nights, you aren't special. He could be in a serious relationship or married. He could be interested in someone else. That's hard to hear. But if he's not serious, you want to know so you can move on and find Mr. Right.

When I tell women who have been involved with men for many months but have never been on a Saturday night date with them, to hold out for Saturday night dates, their relationships often fizzle. In some cases, the women later found out these men—who they thought they were exclusive with—were married or had another significant relationship.

Just because a man comes over for dinner and sex during the week and involves you in his life by doing errands with you, that doesn't mean he's serious about you. You may think it's a good sign early on to be involved in a man's day-to-day life, but in reality, seeing a man during the week but not on Saturday nights is a bad sign. Often what happens in these situations is a man drops off, and a woman will get angry at him. But the signs were there.

What A Legit Excuse Looks Like

A guy who doesn't want to spend Saturday night with you may offer a host of excuses as to what he's doing instead. These excuses include that he's coming down with a cold, spending time with family members, or traveling. There are endless excuses guys give. Sometimes they're true, but many times they aren't.

Legitimate excuses are when a man has custody of his children or he has to work or he's extremely ill. (Although I often find that men who are under the weather will make the date if they like the woman a lot. They practically have to be laid up in bed, unable to move, to miss a date with their Miss Right.)

A male friend of mine, Adam, 43, agrees with the importance of holding out for Saturday nights, saying, "Guys can be sneaky. When they aren't with you Saturday night, it's probably because there's another person involved." Adam is a nice guy, but he knows guys.

When a man has a good excuse for why he can't be with you, he'll usually tell you his reason. A serious contender typically doesn't leave you wondering. He might say, "This Saturday I'm with my daughters, but next Saturday they're with their mom, so I would love to take you out next

Saturday night." Or he'll hire a babysitter. Many men who are deeply interested will get a babysitter, even if it's for a few hours, because it's "too long" to wait another week to see you. If a man doesn't get a babysitter, though, don't be angry. He may not get to see his children much and wants to be with them because it's one of the few nights he gets to see them.

Exceptions To Saturday Night

If a guy works every single Saturday night or has custody of his children every single Saturday or if Saturday nights don't work for you for similar reasons, he'll ask to see you on another night. In that case, Friday is the next best date night.

Also, when it's a blind date or a first online date, it doesn't matter when you go. In this case, the initial meeting can be at any time or any day. When you've never met someone before and don't know if there's chemistry, there's no need to waste the prime real estate of a Saturday night. Fit them in on a less special day and time and make it a quick meet-and-greet type date. For example, it can be a quick coffee during the day or an after-work drink.

If you've been dating a man for many months and he's doing everything right, you can possibly add in another day during the week or add in a day for a special occasion, but Saturday should be your primary date every week. (See

Chapter 6 for more on that.)

The Bottom Line

You want to be the Saturday night girl. By holding out for Saturday nights, you weed out Mr. Wrongs and get a beautiful courtship.

If a man you just started dating doesn't ask you out for Saturday nights, turn everything else down. This way, he's forced to ask you out for Saturday night if he wants to see you. Depending on how he handles this, you can tell whether he's serious about you. If he's not serious about you, he may drop off or give lame excuses for why he can't be with you on Saturday night.

There are legitimate reasons why a man can't be on a date with you on Saturday night. The main ones include that he's working that night or that he needs to take care of his children. If a man isn't available on Saturday nights with a legitimate excuse — and he likes you a lot — he usually makes it clear to you why he isn't available.

Dream *Girl* Dialogue

If a man asks you out for non-Saturday night dates (after the initial meeting), turn him down. If he asks you out for a Friday, say, **"Oh, sounds fun, but I have plans Friday."**

If he picks a Saturday afternoon museum date or a Sunday night football game, nicely turn him down with, **"I'd like to, but I have plans."** Continue doing that until he asks for Saturday night. A guy who likes you enough figures out what he has to do to see you.

Sometimes, when you turn multiple weekday dates down, a man will say, "Tell me what works for you."

The best way to handle this is to say, **"During the week isn't good for me."** This is the truth for most busy women I know — you're juggling jobs, family, friends, and coffee and drink dates with other men. Even if you can make it one of those days, it's still not good for you, as you need to find out if you're the "Saturday night girl." You're serious about finding a good guy and weeding out the wrong guys. Then, continue to turn everything down until he asks for Saturday night.

Some women ask if they can cut to the chase and tell a guy that Saturday is their only night available. While it can be easier to get a Saturday night date that way, it's better when the man asks you out on his own for that special night. Just like with other aspects of courtship, you want the man to lead.

CHAPTER 5

Men Like to Be in Charge

A Man May Be Flattered if You Approach Him First, But You Must Let Him Lead

Let a man make the first move and every subsequent move.

By letting a man lead, a woman sees what a man is capable of giving. Like the advice in other chapters, this tip allows you to have a beautiful romantic courtship, and it's an excellent screening tool. You see who is interested in you and who wants you in their lives.

Don't listen to men who tell you men love it when a woman asks them out. Of course they love it. They're flattered. It makes it easier for them to have sex, too. Lazy men, in particular, love women who ask them out.

When a woman is too easy to get, a man won't always turn her down. He may even ask her out again. But when a woman takes the lead in a romantic relationship, it will emasculate a man. He'll value her much less and won't treat her as well. Men love mystery and challenge, and it's more fun for them when they're figuring out how they're going to ask you out and wondering whether you'll say yes. The suspense is exciting and a thrill. If you ask a man out, the mystery fizzles fast, and the courtship is over. You become more like a family member or a friend or a casual hook-up. (Yes, you want to be a member of his family and his closest friend eventually, but that's for later down the road.) When you're dating, you don't want things to turn casual too quickly.

Sometimes women feel they're being mean by letting a man take the lead. They think they should do half the work in initiating a relationship. Their reasoning is that by letting the man do all the work, they're not being fair. They think the man will see them as selfish for not putting in an equal effort. But remember, men and women think differently: men like mystery and women like stability. Men enjoy and thrive on the chase.

When you let men lead and learn to receive, you're embracing your feminine energy. When you become better at being the receiver, you automatically give less during the pursuit and wait to receive what he's capable of giving. If a man doesn't give, you learn a lot. You learn he's not going to be a giver. Accept this is who he is and that he won't change, so it's best to move on.

Receiving isn't about taking advantage of a man. It's an essential part of courtship.

When you're married, things change, and you can give to a man in different ways. During marriage, a man will still lead. But you don't need to let him chase you like he did during courtship. During marriage, you're on one another's team. He's already conquered you. You've already laid the groundwork for a successful marriage by allowing him to court you. All that hard work during courtship paid off, and you have a man who loves and adores you. You'll do things for him in marriage that you wouldn't do in courtship, such as make meals for him, put him first, and be available when he needs you. When married, you make his life easy, and you make him a priority, unlike dating, when you are harder to get.

During courtship you let Mr. Right lead as you trust that a relationship will unfold the way it should, with no nagging or forceful direction from you. (See Chapter 12.) You should accept him for who he is and let go of the fantasy of how you think your ideal mate should act and what he should look like — without sacrificing what's really important to you. Often when women do this, they get someone even better for them than they imagined.

Many women struggle with letting a man lead. Others have no idea how to encourage this to happen. They botch courtship because their masculine energy creeps in, unknowingly and even subconsciously, and this confuses men. They may agree that a man should make the first move, yet they may eventually take over, thinking they're being helpful.

For example, say a man meets a woman at an outdoor concert. He asks her out for the following Saturday night. He takes her phone number, and he says he'll call to confirm. On Wednesday, she still hasn't heard from him, so she texts him to make sure they are still on and she suggests a fun outdoor place near her for dinner. She thinks she's making it easier for both of them by getting the date all ironed out. But in reality, she's doing more harm than good.

And there are some women who don't think it's fair that they can't take the lead entirely. They think they should be able to ask a man out and drive a relationship forward. After all, men and women are equal, right? It's true women are equal to men, but when it comes to romantic relationships, men and women are biologically different. Men want to lead and run the show. It all needs to come from the man. Otherwise he may do something to please you in the moment, but because he never had any intention of making a move himself, he won't drive the relationship forward.

Men are also very visual and have types. (More on this in Chapter 16.) When you assist a man in asking you out or if you directly ask him out, you'll never know if he wanted to be with you. He may have accepted to be polite. He may just go along with it because you made it easy. You need to see how he behaves on his own, without prodding. This is how you weed out men who aren't that interested. It saves you time and energy and keeps you in control of your dating life. This way, you only end up with men who like you, and you won't get into emotionally devastating situations with ambivalent men.

If he isn't calling you or asking you out on dates, you aren't his dream girl. It's harsh, I know, but it's better to know the truth so you don't waste time and so you find your Mr. Right sooner rather than later.

There are times when you'll have to stand up for yourself if a man does something unacceptable, or when you'll need to give a man an ultimatum if he's taking too long to commit. (More on this in Chapters 18 and 22.) But beyond that, let a man initiate everything. He needs to ask you out. He must initiate texts and calls unless there's a special exception, which is rare in all honesty. Many clients rarely, if ever, initiate texts with their boyfriends. One client who went away with her boyfriend of nine months for a ski weekend, took a quick walk while he was in the shower, and got lost. She was scared because she didn't know where she was, so she initiated a text, "Hey, I think I'm lost."

"That was the only time I ever had to initiate a text with him," she said. "There was never a need, even while we were planning our wedding, for me to initiate texts. He initiated all the texts and when there was something I wanted to run by him, such as a question about the guest list, I would bring it up after he called or texted or when we were on a date. It worked out beautifully and our wedding planning and wedding went smoothly and was beyond magical."

Let him initiate kissing, romance, sex, and most everything. He must plan the proposal. Let him pick the restaurant and the entertainment throughout courtship. Usually what happens is he'll learn what your favorite restaurants and entertainment preferences are and will plan with those in mind. Eventually when you're married, you can of course suggest restaurants and entertainment and even plan outings, but that's for later on down the road when you're on one another's team.

Another reason never to make the initial move with a man is because you don't know if a man is married, engaged, or seriously involved with someone. Just because a guy isn't wearing a ring doesn't mean he's single. Some married men don't wear rings, and committed men who are in serious relationships or engaged don't wear rings, either. His initiative is what shows you his availability.

Women Can't Have It Both Ways

When you make the first move or help it along, you risk being the driver of that relationship going forward.

You'll be the one planning Valentine's Day, wondering where your romantic bouquets are. You'll be acting with masculine energy, and you'll wonder why he's not stepping up. You'll wonder why you need to make all the decisions and moves in the relationship. It's because you took the lead initially, so that will inevitably be your role. You may even start wondering if he cares for you or loves you.

You can't pursue a man during the initial stages of a relationship and then all of a sudden tell him, "Okay, so now I want you to pursue me more, show me lots of affection, and make all the decisions."

You're being selfish and unrealistic if you feel you deserve to have it both ways. The same way your relationship started — with you doing all the work — is how the relationship will continue.

Even if he's attracted to you initially, but you pushed the relationship along by making subsequent overtures, some of the romantic tension will be lost. When he doesn't have to work hard to get you, his excitement level isn't as strong.

Beware Of Lazy Men

One thing that may happen in the dating trenches is you'll run across men who want you to do all the work. These guys tend to be lazy or passive. Or they may not be that interested in you. Either way, they aren't going to give you the relationship dreams are made of.

These relationships — if they ever get off the ground — tend to be disasters. These men want to be the prize. They're often looking for an ego boost, not a real relationship. A man who wants a woman to pursue him is looking for the easy way out. He wants someone to make it effortless for him. This is a predictor of a bad boyfriend — one who doesn't provide for or protect his girlfriend well, one who's not committed to her.

Lazy men may say in their online profiles that they love when women ask them out. Beware of men who say this. When you ask a man out, it flatters their ego. But they may be married and are only online for an ego-stroking. Some men are online simply to collect photos of women. Or they're bored and looking for a pen pal, not a real relationship.

If you wait for a man to ask you out, you'll bypass all the time wasters. If he's not pursuing, you need to let him go and wait for the one who wants to woo you. When a man doesn't pursue, it may be painful at first — especially if you've been on several dates and feel like you have a connection with the man. But realize he's doing you a favor because he's making space for Mr. Right to take his place. Hold out for a man who innately knows he must pursue you and who wants to win you over.

When a man sees you as his dream girl, he's all in. You don't need to convince him.

Staring Means Nothing

Sometimes women say, "I know he really likes me. He's always talking to me and watching me," or "Every time I go to that bar, he's staring at me. I know he's interested." He may be interested, but unless he makes moves to ask you out and court you properly, he's not interested *enough*. You deserve better.

Also, he could be staring for a different reason than you think. He may think you're pretty, but if he does nothing, it's not worth getting excited about. He may not like your look. You may not be his type. Or even if you're his type, there may be another reason. He may have a girlfriend. He could be married. He might not be motivated to date for whatever reason.

Prince Charming Turns Into A Frog

Tess, 29, dated a guy, Rod, 34, who started off as Prince Charming, but things changed after a few months. Of particular concern was that Rod started to get annoyed that he was having to plan all the dates. He asked Tess to plan the next date. She said, "Okay," and then called me. I told her to ignore his request to plan the date and wait it out. She asked, "What if he never calls me again?" I replied, "Then you have your answer as to where the relationship is going."

He continued to call her for Saturday night dates, but things didn't go smoothly. When he picked her up one Saturday night, he again asked her to plan the date. She told him she was fine with him planning it. He rolled his eyes and said, "Okay, but pick a restaurant." She picked one that she liked, and he immediately told her it was too expensive.

The expense wasn't the issue, because it was the type of restaurant they'd been going to during their courtship. It didn't cost more or less. My sense was that he was finding things wrong because he wanted to break up but didn't know how else to express it. He was trying to throw a wrench in the relationship. Asking her to plan their dates was a smokescreen.

Often when guys feel something's not working out, they act difficult because they want you to break up with them. Many men find it hard to tell you directly that they don't see a future. (See more on this in Chapter 21.) Soon after Rod started asking Tess to plan dates, he said something verbally abusive to her, and she broke up with him.

When a guy is into you, he takes the initiative to move a relationship forward. He doesn't ask you to plan dates, which is what Rod did. He'll pay attention to your preferences. A good guy wants to know what kind of food you like and what your favorite restaurants are. He listens, asks questions, and makes plans with your likes and dislikes in mind.

But he'll run the show. That is, if you allow him to. He'll call and ask you out on dates. He'll plan the dates and pay. He'll be the first to introduce you to family and friends, the first to talk about the future, and the first to make romantic overtures.

If you get a man by pursuing, that's fine if that is what you want, but it won't lead to a happy marriage or a serious loving relationship that reflects the differences between men and women.

The Bottom Line

Let a man make the first move and every other move. This is an essential part of courtship. While you're letting the man lead, you're receiving and seeing what he's capable of giving. This puts you in control in more ways than you think, because when you let a man lead, you can tell if he's into you because he's moving the relationship forward. The men who don't lead are usually not interested enough. Or they are passive men who want a woman to take the lead.

Also by letting a man lead, you're allowing him to chase you, which gives him a thrill and a challenge, and it will likely cause him to treat you better.

Dream *Girl* Dialogue

Here's how to respond when a man asks you out. I've also included dialogue for how to respond when a man turns the tables and tries to get you to plan the date.

When a guy leads, responding and receiving is easy. When he asks you out online or even in person, all you need to say is, **"Sure!"** or **"Sounds good!"** You can talk more on the date.

If he asks for suggestions on where to go on a date, you can say, **"What are you thinking?"** You want to see what he's going to pick without you suggesting or prodding. If he presses you for preferences, you can give them.

There are times, like the scenario with Tess, when a guy asks you to plan dates. This isn't the greatest sign, as a man is asking you to take on the masculine role. If he asks this in person, look at him, dumbfounded, like you never heard such a question before and say, **"Plan the date?"** Don't say it angrily, more like you don't understand the question. And don't plan the date. This isn't courtship.

If he persists, don't get into an argument. Best to say, **"Hmmm, let me think about it."** Then think about it for a long time, and definitely don't do it. This isn't the greatest sign of a pursuer, so it could end here.

If he asks how the date planning is going, say, **"Oh,**

haven't had a chance." If he wants to see you, he'll figure out what he needs to do to see you, and in this case, what he needs to do is plan the date himself.

CHAPTER 6

Less is More With Men

Why Pacing a Relationship is Key—and How to Do It

Do less. Go slow.

Although going fast and doing more works in other areas of your life, when it comes to dating, doing less and taking it slow is always better. It allows you to leapfrog ahead in any dating situation. When you go slow, you get to the finish line quicker because you weed out the wrong men fast, and you get Mr. Right to fall hard and fast for you. When you do less and go slow, you're pacing the relationship. This is how you leave the right man wanting more.

When you pace a relationship, you weed out dreaded time wasters. They drop off fast. By pacing a relationship, you also screen for the love-bomber type who needs to go fast and get close to you quickly because he's too insecure to go slow.

When you pace a relationship by doing less and going slow, you're also much more mysterious to a man. He's on the edge of his seat, wondering about you all the time. You're allowing a man to chase you. A romantic relationship is more fun for a healthy man if you give him space and if he gets to unwrap you slowly, learning more about you as the relationship progresses. It keeps the courtship process fun and the romantic fire burning longer. Anything intense that happens fast kills the challenge. You need to give a man breathing room.

I've noticed certain celebrity wives who captured the world's most eligible bachelors, such as Amal Clooney, Meghan Markle, Jessica Seinfeld, and Carolyn Bessette, seemed to operate on the less-is-more principle. Based on what I read about them in the press, they didn't act all "fangirl" over their celebrity partner. Ultimately because of that, these VIP men had to have these women. They couldn't get them so easily, so they wanted them.

Whether you want to date and marry a VIP, the man next door, or someone else, doing less rather than more works with men.

Pacing a relationship is a gift you're giving to a man, even when he's pressuring to see you more. When you don't give a man space, you kill the thrill.

Some women think it's good when a relationship becomes casual and familiar early on. They want the relationship wrapped up in a week. They also want him to know they like him, so he's not guessing. They think they're hurting him by holding back. They're attracted to a man's surface characteristics and want to rush the getting-to-know-you part by sharing everything right away. They think it will get them closer to a man, and it will. But this type of closeness isn't healthy when it happens too quickly. Plus, it doesn't keep a man's interest.

In fact, when a man's nervous about you and wonders

whether you like him as much as he likes you, he's enjoying himself because, as I've said, men love a chase. When it gets too casual too soon, he gets bored.

Men like a challenge. Even when men tell you they want it to be easy. Even when they complain you're too hard to get. They might say things when they start dating you like, "Waiting a week to see you is too long. I want to see you more than once a week."

Don't listen. Well, listen, of course—this is good intel, and is a good sign that he wants to see you more—but don't give in, because if he starts seeing you more than once a week early on, he'll take you for granted. Eventually, of course, you want to get close to a man and see him every day (marriage). But a long-term relationship or marriage is better when the courtship is slower, so keep it to once a week in the first three months or more.

You want a man to dream about you, wondering what it will be like to sleep with you. He'll fantasize all week about what you'll be wearing. He'll wonder what your shiny hair will look like and how you'll smell. He'll wonder whether you'll kiss him or allow him to do more. He'll wonder what it will be like to sleep with you. (Did I say that already?)

When he's with you, a man feels like his rare time with you is unforgettable, and he'll use phrases like, "You're special," and as you get closer, he'll say things like, "I want to make love with you so badly."

A big part of this is because you're behaving in a way that makes you mysterious to him. He sees you as different.

When a woman doesn't understand men and doesn't

pace the relationship, it can end as quickly as it started. A man may stop calling or act cranky. He may tell you he's working longer at the office or that he's catering to family members who are visiting or he's in the hospital or a number of other excuses.

Some men may be honest and say they need space. It's one of the worst feelings in the world when you're attracted to a guy who was also into you, and then he starts pulling away. The less-is-more approach will help you avoid all this pain—and it will make Mr. Right more ardent.

When you pace a relationship, men use words like "beguiling" to describe you. My client, Ledimar, 35, from Brazil, said that her husband told her after proposing, "I've been hypnotized by your beguiling beauty since the day we met. I missed you so much during the week. I realized if I proposed, I would get to see you every day."

Pacing a relationship with a new man you like can be hard, especially when you're attracted to him, and he's all over you. When a man comes on strong and a relationship gets hot and heavy fast, it feels so good and can be oh so tricky to navigate. It's easy to get carried away. It's hard not to see him all the time, especially if he tells you how much he likes you and is asking to see you frequently. After all, the attention feels amazing, and it's hot and sexy and fun. It can be difficult for many women to refrain from telling a guy how strongly they feel about him. If you don't understand men, you may respond to his comments about how much he likes you by giving him equally flattering comments.

(See Chapter 14.) But practice receiving here, too.

A man will want to see you frequently in the early stages of a relationship. Guys often fall harder at first. Many women—unless they understand men well—reciprocate a man's overtures early on, just as fast and intensely as he makes them. The woman thinks she has a cosmic connection because she feels so good. But then the bottom drops, and he pulls away.

Women who don't understand men have no idea what's happening. To avoid this situation, women need to put on the breaks. When a man pursues ardently in the beginning and then pulls back, it's not always because he's a jerk. It could be that he gets too much from a woman and realizes, "Oh jeez, I need some space."

Women are nurturing types and feel that if they give love and are open and honest with a man early on, the man will fall deeply in love. Women often get confused and think that what works for women works for men. But it doesn't. Men are fueled by the opposite. They're more aroused when you're not so easily conquered. They want that chase.

See A Man Once A Week

As discussed before, the best way to pace a relationship is to only see a guy on Saturday nights for at least the first few months, or even longer depending on your unique situation. If a good man makes it through the first three months (12 Saturday nights)—driving to your area, paying, and hanging in there even though you're not ready to sleep with him — you've most likely got a serious contender. (This is a great sign, although not a done deal.) This can be a good time to start seeing him twice a week.

There are times during those first few months when you can see him more than once a week, but you should reserve those times for special circumstances. Like, for example, if you start dating in January, and in February he wants to see you on Valentine's Day, which falls during the week, and also on Saturday night. In that case, you can see him twice that week because Valentine's Day is special.

Another key reason to pace a relationship is because getting all hot and heavy with a man early on, seeing him multiple times a week, is wasting time that should be spent on yourself. Many of you are busy and filled with responsibilities — jobs, children, and other family obligations. You're also multi-dating. (See Chapter 8.) Focusing too much on one man you've just met, who hasn't proven himself to you, isn't smart.

Men Like The Hard-To-Get Woman

Men love to brag to friends and family about how their girlfriends or wives were initially hard to get. Or how their girlfriends didn't like to talk on the phone or text much.

My client, Hanna, 46, from Italy, overheard her fiancé, Ryan, 51, telling his sister, "She never texted me. And when she replied, she texted two words!" He was laughing when he said it, proud he got the girl who was so hard to reach.

Eve, 42, is another example of what happens when you text a guy less. Eve said she felt bad because she only texted her boyfriend back infrequently. Then she emailed me, saying, "It's working. He keeps sending me poems and is making all these amazing Saturday night plans."

A man appreciates that you're different than most women and aren't blowing up his phone. He's pleased you're respecting his need for space. You understand him, and that's appealing to a man. Some men may complain you don't text or call enough, which is a good problem to have. It means he wants more of you.

I've been with men when they received massive text fests from women. One friend, Tristian, 44, showed me texts from a woman, saying, "This lady is crazy." The texts were aggressive and wordy, and he only answered her with a few words or a sentence, and she wrote several paragraphs back to him each time.

"She's telling me about some drama at work, and I think she's trying to be entertaining, but it's annoying. Can't she get the hint by my one-word answers that I'm not amused? There is no way I'm going out on a date with her," Tristian said.

When you text a man more than he texts you, or even if your texting efforts are equal, you become less special and mysterious. So when you're dating a man who asks you to text or call him more, don't do it. Of course you can reply to date-related texts, but beyond that, save most of the communicating for the date.

The good guys who like you will respect that you're putting on the brakes, and while they may grumble a bit, they'll keep trying to see you. On some subconscious level, they'll be thanking you.

My client, Talisa, 50, from Dubai, said her boyfriend, Jon, 50, got annoyed at her because she rarely texted him back and was too busy during the week to see him. But then as they got more serious, he told her how much he liked her and he thanked her. He said, "I like how you handled things by taking it slow." He said he appreciated how fun and exciting their first few months together were. He described her as special and different than other women he'd dated. Men may not consciously realize this, and many women don't get this, but men fall in love during the absences.

A little annoyance or a normal amount of anger can be good, because it means he cares and wants to see you more. There may be times when you pace a relationship and a guy gets livid or complains nonstop in a mean way. If he throws a fit and calls you names, that's a man who can't control his anger, and it's a big red flag.

Leave Him Wanting More

Men get bored quickly, even with a sizzling hot model. The person who texts, calls, talks, or does more is the person who cares more, and until you know where you stand with this guy, you don't want to be the one who cares more. Even when he cares for you, stay chill.

You want to be the receiver, and you want him to be the giver when courting. Some women wonder, "How will he know I like him if I'm always receiving from him? Don't I have to give back?" The way to give back to a man is to be receptive to his pursuit. Say yes to dates, be happy, and look hot on dates. Smiling is great, too.

Here are tips to keep you in the less-is-more mode. These tips will keep the chase going and keep the mystery alive:

- End every date first.
- End phone calls first.
- Text less than him, and don't double text.
- Don't text back in nanoseconds.
- Don't get into massive texting exchanges. Try to respond only to date-related texts for the most part.
- See him once a week — on Saturday night — for the first few months. (As discussed in Chapter 4.)
- Don't accept exclusivity too soon. (More on this in Chapter 8.)
- Delay revealing your feelings too soon (wait for him to tell you how he feels). He should be the one gushing about you. You can reciprocate on occasion, but for the most part, play it cool, and always do less than him.
- Delay sleeping with him right away. (As discussed

in Chapter 2.)
- Don't accept last-minute dates. (For more on this, see Chapter 18 and Chapter 21.)

You may think a man will drop off if you adhere to these principles. But the right man won't be deterred. When it's the right guy, this is the recipe for a beautiful courtship.

My client, Tiffany, 35, from Colorado, said her fiancé, Mike, 39, told her that when she left early on Sunday mornings after spending Saturday night at his house, he would call his brother, mystified by her behavior. Mike would beg her to stay so they could spend Sundays together, but for the first month after they started sleeping together, she had a yoga class. Mike was annoyed, but this is the kind of annoyed you want. Even though Mike complained, he treated Tiffany like gold and proposed in nine months.

The Bottom Line

Keep the less-is-more mantra in the back of your mind at all times in dating situations. When it comes to men, less is more and going slow is good. While instant gratification feels good in the moment, it can do more damage in the end.

This less-is-more philosophy won't work if you're with Mr. Wrong, but that's the whole point. This concept allows you to see when a man's feelings are genuine. It also makes Mr. Right more ardent. I realize this can be hard for women, especially women who are used to making things happen in their professional lives. What you must realize, however, is that what works professionally won't work in a romantic relationship with a healthy, masculine man. You may even feel mean when holding back. But the more you apply these principles in real life, the more you'll see how well they work. A good man in love responds well to the less-is-more approach.

Dream *Girl* Dialogue

Often in the beginning stages of dating, a man will push for more than Saturday night dates. He may want to see you five days a week or even more. Nicely turn him down. A simple sentence like this works, **"I'd like to, but I can't on Wednesday."**

If he persists and asks, "Don't you want to go on a date? I really like you a lot. Seeing you only Saturday isn't enough. I want to see you more." You can reply, **"Yes, but weekdays are busy."** At some point a few months in, if he's persisting and wants to see you more than Saturday and appears to be doing everything right, you can say, **"This week's just busy. It's not a convenient week."** It shows you're softening up and not saying never.

Saying you're busy is not a lie. Weekdays are tough for most women. It's a lot to give a guy in the beginning. It works to his advantage, not yours. It takes time away from multi-dating, which is healthy, plus it also takes time from your job and, if you're a single mom, from your family life. (Read more in Chapter 8.)

You're not being rude or selfish. You're taking care of yourself. If he's the right man, he'll respect this. He'll stick it out, and when he's proven himself, you can add in more days. If he fades away, you'll be so happy you spent as little time as possible with the cad that got away.

Another aspect of pacing is ending dates first. Here's a good script for ending the date politely, **"Oh, wow, I have a big day tomorrow. I guess we should get going."**

When he asks what you're doing on certain days, like Sunday, there's no need to tell him in detail. Be vague. These are good answers: **"I have a busy day"** or **"Meeting some friends."**

When a man starts telling you how much he loves you, your first reaction should be one of receiving. You should smile and say, **"Thanks!"** If he's a good guy who's sticking around, he'll say, "I love you" again, and in that case, you can reciprocate with an **"I love you."** But only if you feel it, and only if you feel he's a good guy who isn't saying "I love you" to get you to have sex with him.

Certainly never say it first. If he talks early on about how intense his feelings are for you, simply smile and say, **"Thanks."** Don't reciprocate early on. His words could be meaningless. Even if he means them, he'll be more enamored if you play it cool. You don't ever want the balance to shift, where you're complimenting him more than he's complimenting you. (See more in Chapter 14.)

You can reciprocate more and more as you start to get to know a man and learn whether he's a good man who has truly fallen for you. But make sure to always give less than him.

(Things will change when you're married. When married, you should be building him up and giving him compliments. When married you'll be on his team and will be able to give much more, and you'll be his biggest supporter. He will be your priority in life. But even in marriage you don't want the balance to shift where you're acting clingy.)

CHAPTER 7

Talk is Cheap

A Man's Actions, Not His Words, Will Show You His Heart

Beware of sweet talk.

Men say a lot of things, but their words don't necessarily mean what they say. If you only listen to a man's words, you can get hurt and waste time. Men's actions are more important than their words, and they'll help you determine when men are genuinely interested in you.

Many women place more importance on words than they should. This is easy to do. Who doesn't want to believe that all the charming, romantic, and loving things a man says are sincere? But when you place too much importance on words, you end up staying stuck, either in fantasy relationships or in a relationship that goes nowhere.

Women fall in love between the ears. They fall for a man's words. Many men know this is true. Sometimes a man who doesn't have serious intentions about a woman takes advantage, using words to win her over so he can sleep with her.

Sometimes a man will have a hard time letting you down easy, so the words he uses don't reflect how he truly feels. It would be great if everything a man said was true. But men aren't always truthful.

"I Love You, But I Don't Want To Date You"

Beatriz, 40, from Barcelona, contacted me because she was confused about a guy she was dating named Javier, 39. She thought they were in a serious relationship, and she was envisioning marrying him. He called her the "love of his life," "amazing," "lovely," and "captivating."

When I pressed Beatriz, I learned she only spent time with Javier when she planned dates. He wasn't around on Saturday nights. She would see him Thursday or Friday nights or on Sundays. She called him and orchestrated the dates, down to the last detail. Javier always said, "Sure," when she called. She was entertaining and knew all the cool restaurants and venues. She was funny, worldly, and articulate. They had fascinating intellectual discussions and deep talks.

But it never turned romantic. If she didn't call him, she never heard from him.

It's crucial to watch a guy's actions, or in this case, the lack of actions. If Beatriz had, she would have saved time and grief. She would have let him go sooner. She likely wouldn't have gotten involved with him in the first place.

Beatriz spoke to Javier first and planned their first meeting. Beatriz thought things were going well at first because Javier kept agreeing to meet her, and she kept getting tripped up on his beautiful words.

She put him on the spot after a few months. "Why don't you ever call me? Why am I always planning our get-togethers?" she asked. That's when he told her she was the "love of my life." Even after she confronted him, he couldn't tell her the truth — that she wasn't the one.

My guess is that Javier didn't want to hurt her feelings. And I'm sure he felt a connection. He might have loved her. But it wasn't romantic love. It was more akin to a relationship between close friends or siblings.

If she wanted to know what he felt about her romantically, she had to stop calling him and stop planning dates. She had to observe his actions. When she finally accepted my advice and stopped contacting him, he faded away. She learned that he had been pursuing someone else the whole time.

Most of the time, it's not effective to put men on the spot, as Beatriz did. In scenarios like this one, you'll find that men aren't always honest.

There are times when you can gently ask questions to get a read on what's going on. (See Chapter 22.) But even in those situations, make sure a man follows up with the right actions. Many times, he'll answer politely, like Javier.

If you don't understand men, you're likely to take their words at face value. A lot of times men say things like this: "We need to get together again," "We would make a great couple," or "You're my soulmate." Then they never follow through with being in the same room as you. This may appear confusing. But it's not complicated. Actions tell the story loud and clear. Even if a man says something warm and loving and feels it in the moment, it doesn't mean he cares enough to follow through. Watch how men respond.

There are also times when a man might say things to make himself sound like a good guy. For example, he might say he loves a woman without makeup. But he ogles and pines over the hot Eva Longoria lookalike who is all made up and dressed to kill. I've heard many men say they don't like it when women wear makeup, but those same men are turned on by it and will ask that woman out if she's their type. I've also noticed that often the men who say, "Women look good without makeup," don't know the reality of what "no makeup" really looks like.

One of my clients, Lisa, 49, told me a story that illustrates how it's best not to always listen to what men say. Lisa said that after a few months of dating Tom, 53, he told her she didn't have to get glammed up for him. So she stopped wearing makeup, thinking he liked the natural look.

Soon after, I got an email from her telling me how they almost got into an accident after a dinner date in a swank part of London. Three women who looked like they stepped out of a Victoria's Secret catalog were walking down the street. Tom turned to look and almost collided with another car. Lisa felt dumpy while he was ogling these women who were all wearing lots of makeup. Lisa didn't say anything to Tom while on that date, but his actions made her feel badly about herself. She vowed she would always wear makeup going forward because she knew she looked and felt better while wearing it. Lisa broke up with Tom because he turned out to be too abrasive and insensitive in general. She never felt like a dream girl around him. Something always felt off when they were together.

Be Wary Of Words In Online Profiles

Just like you need to be careful of words in real life, be cautious online. Take online dating profiles with a grain of salt. All is revealed through a man's actions while dating him.

There are even times when a man's online dating profile will say the exact opposite of the truth. He may say, "I don't like drama in a relationship." A man who says that may be doing so because his relationships are drama-filled. On some level, he might like drama, even though it causes him trouble and even though he thinks he doesn't want it. He could be in therapy because he's attracted to drama and dysfunction.

Sometimes men bring up thorny issues because these issues are at the forefront of their minds and they've been problems in prior relationships. These men may think they're being honest. But there are many instances where men don't turn out as described.

One client dated a guy who had written in his online dating profile that he was easygoing and down to earth. His exterior was nice, but underneath he was cranky and entitled. He may have thought he was amiable, but once she got to know him, he was mean in a passive-aggressive way.

He skipped her birthday and ghosted her after they spent many months together.

When Words Matter

While actions are more important than words, words matter. Everything—his actions, his words, how you feel inside when you're with a guy—is valuable intel. Focus more on actions because flattering words are nothing unless they're backed up by actions.

But words are particularly important when they're mean or negative. That's when you should believe a man's words. If he says something like, "Your sister is way prettier than you," "I've cheated on every girlfriend I ever had, and I don't believe in monogamy," or "My ex-girlfriend was so much better than you in bed," you should *run*.

A guy who is falling in love, who envisions a future, and who sees you as his dream girl would never utter any of those sentences. A man doesn't talk like that to his dream girl because he doesn't want to risk losing her.

The Bottom Line

When you want to know how a man feels about you, consider his actions or lack of actions more than his words. Sweet talk is nice. If it's there along with actions, that's awesome and a beautiful thing. I'm all for expressive and loving men. But the right words don't always lead to loving actions and commitment. That's why you need to watch the follow-through. Also note that words from a man can be extremely concerning when they are negative.

Dream *Girl* Dialogue

While dating, you'll be on the receiving end of sweet talk. Some of it will likely be sincere and some of it won't be, and you may not know at the time. Either way, receive the compliment gracefully by smiling and saying, **"Thanks."**

But don't be so blinded by words that you ignore the follow-through.

When you suspect you're on the receiving end of false flattery, there's no need to argue or tell a man he's being fake. Use your energy to find Mr. Right. There's never any need to take on the world and cause drama.

CHAPTER 8

Keep Your Options Open

Be Like a Guy and Multi-Date

Don't take yourself off the market too soon.

This is one of the few times I'll tell you to act more like a man. It's quite healthy to multi-date, and it saves time. It softens the blow if you meet a man who seems like the Mr. Right you've been waiting for your whole life, yet he turns out to be totally and utterly Mr. Wrong. This way, you have options and more control over your dating life.

Love and lust can blind you, and it's easy to focus on one man right away. When a man is saying and doing all the right things, it feels so good and becomes easy to think, "He has to be *the one*."

Even if a relationship seems like it's going well, I tell clients to continue to date others. This may seem like a cynical way of looking at love, but it's not. It's smart, and gets you to that special someone much faster, whether it's the main man you're dating or another one waiting in the wings.

Too many women are too nice in the early stages of dating. After dating a guy for a few dates, a woman may feel that he's being so good to her, so sweet, that it would be rude to continue to date others. She is afraid the guy will see her online and get angry. So she shuts down her online dating accounts. Fast forward three months, the woman realizes the guy isn't as nice as she thought, and he's dating others. Meanwhile, she wasted time.

Even when you dread the thought of that blind date your friend is setting up, don't stop multi-dating. A man who seems great early on can pull back, and the pain of the breakup is magnified because you're home alone on a Saturday night. No plans. No men lined up to take you out. It's easier to get back out there if you stay in the game. There might even be a serious contender in the wings from all that multi-dating.

Multi-dating saves you time on this journey to find Mr. Right. Who knows, maybe one of the men you're dating will turn out to be someone extra special and rise to the cream of the crop faster than the main man?

Sometimes when you're distracted by a love gone wrong, you're more appealing to a new guy. You're getting over one guy, so you pay less attention to the new guy in your multi-dating orbit, and that sets in motion the essential chase. Multi-dating is a win-win.

There will be a time, of course, when you can get off the apps and sites and stop looking. But make sure you think long and hard about giving a man exclusivity too soon.

Sometimes a man will ask for exclusivity after a second or third date. That's too soon. You should stay on the market until he's proven that he's a serious contender, which is something that you can't tell after only a few dates.

I can't give blanket advice telling you the exact moment, because everyone's circumstances are different. But generally if a man asks for exclusivity three months in, after doing all the right things, it's a good time to accept exclusivity and stop dating others.

Sometimes a man who really likes you just assumes you're exclusive and never asks for exclusivity, and one day he ends up proposing. If you're getting a good feeling from this man, and he's doing all the right things, it's okay to sleep with him after 12 or so dates, if you feel ready, even if he hasn't asked to be exclusive.

But because he hasn't cemented your relationship yet by explicitly asking, play the field. By playing the field, I don't think you should sleep with many men. You should sleep with the main man but still go on coffee, drink, and dinner dates with others. If he never asks to be exclusive, it's smart to go on dates with others until he does commit to you.

Some women ask whether they should confirm with a guy before they sleep with him, asking whether he's sleeping with other women. The answer is a big NO. First of all, asking this question sounds desperate. Also, as you know, men's words don't always tell the whole story. Even if a man asks to be exclusive and tells you that he's not sleeping with anyone else, he could be lying.

Don't fret though—by the time you've reached the 3-month mark (12 consistent Saturday nights) you're likely getting a good or bad feeling from the man and whether he's smitten. If you're getting a bad feeling, you shouldn't sleep with him, of course. But usually after 12 Saturday consistent nights, where he's driving to you and paying for dates, a man is typically really into you or else he would have dropped off. Oftentimes you'll get a good feeling about how a man feels about you through other ways, too.

Such as, his friend pulls you into a private conversation and says, "I haven't seen him this in love with someone before. He's really into you." Or the man you're dating will tell you he wants you to meet his teenage children and sets up a time for you to meet them. Or he may push to see you more and more during the week, telling you how he sees a future with you. This is a very good sign. (Sure, as I've said, some men lie to get you to sleep with them, and your guy could be lying about future plans. But a man in love brings up the future, too.)

I realize multi-dating is hard to do if your heart is with the main Saturday night man. But even in cases where it looks extremely promising and a man is doing and saying all the right things, the bottom can fall out. Some men can't commit fully to anyone. Some men are just looking for a girlfriend and have no intention of anything serious or long-term. Some men ask for exclusivity early, only to become emotionally abusive.

I'm often asked what to do if there are two promising men chasing you and both are asking for Saturday night. (By the way, this is a great problem to have!) Basically, do your best to figure out who you like most and who treats you best, and he's your main Saturday night man. Then, see the other man on Friday night, which is the second-best date night.

Be A Smart Multi-Dater

One client, Nelly, 44, from Scotland, was dating Ian,

49, who she liked a lot. She was attracted to him, and they seemed to get along well and have common interests and morals. He always drove more than one hour to pick her up and then drop her back home after their dates. Even though he had a lot of baggage and a lot on his plate with work and family, he consistently saw her every Saturday night and introduced her to his family. They did start sleeping together after three months because she got the feeling he liked her and wasn't seeing anyone else, although he never asked to be exclusive.

Because she never quite knew for sure how committed he was to her, she didn't take herself off the market. Even though she liked Ian and hoped he would step up, she stayed online—on multiple dating sites and apps. She went out for drink dates with other men, although she never slept with anyone else because Ian was the main guy. She was hoping their relationship would flower properly.

Nelly waited for Valentine's Day for a final sign. What a man does on your birthday and Valentine's Day offers valuable information about how he feels about you and what kind of man he is. He skipped the day, and when they were out on their Saturday night date, he didn't give her a gift or tell her, "Happy Valentine's Day." The only time he acknowledged the date was when he looked over at other couples who were celebrating it, and said, "What a stupid holiday." She started a conversation about their relationship and never saw him after that. He did text her a few times, late at night, probably bored and hoping for a hookup. She ignored those texts. Thankfully she was multi-dating the whole time she was seeing him and had other dates lined up. That made the breakup less difficult emotionally.

"I wished I had dated even more aggressively than I did, looking back. I should have gone on more dates during the weekdays when I wasn't with him," she told me. This story has a happy ending, though. Two months after Ian dropped out of her life, Nelly went on a blind date with a handsome architect named Brendan, 49, who recently moved to her town. They clicked right away, and within three months, he asked to be exclusive. She told him she'd think about it, and then when he asked her again, she accepted. Six months in, he bought a new house, and asked Nelly for her input, because he told her, "I want this to be something you're comfortable living in." Two months later, on her birthday, he proposed with a solitaire-shaped ring.

The Bottom Line

Men can be mercurial early on. Because you don't know for sure until many months in where a man's head is at, it is smart to multi-date. Men say and do many things that make it seem like they see a future with you, but sometimes they pull back. You don't want to be devastated when and if this happens. You want to move on fast to someone who is right for you, and the best way to do that is to multi-date. When multi-dating, it's good to keep the main man on Saturday nights and then date others for drinks, coffee, or dinner, on other days.

Some women say they don't have time to multi-date. Just

realize, if you're serious about finding love, and softening the blow in case your Saturday night guy is actually Mr. Wrong, do your best to find time to multi-date because it saves you more time in the end. The way I advocate dating doesn't take up much time in the early stages. When you're pacing relationships, early on you aren't spending an overwhelming amount of time with any man.

Initially you're going slow and pacing all your dates, so it shouldn't be hard to fit a few hours in for Saturday night dates and one or more quick meet-and-greet type dates or even a short dinner date with another man. If finding Mr. Right is your main goal, then you should make it a priority. This won't go on forever. It's simply a means to an end.

You should delay exclusivity, never accepting after only a few dates. Mr. Wrong might run from this, but you don't want Mr. Wrong in your life. A good rule of thumb is to accept at around three months of dating, which is typically 12 dates, but situations are different for everyone and you may require a private coaching consult with me to iron this out.

Dream *Girl* Dialogue

When a man asks for exclusivity too soon, a great script to use is, **"Wow, let me think about it."** Then think about it until you're sure. This is a good script to use as a delaying tactic. If a man seems to be doing all the right things for three months and you like him, that could be a good time to accept.

When you're ready to accept exclusivity, all you need to do is smile and say, **"Okay!"** That is short and sweet and upbeat. Don't give him a long talk about how happy you are—even if you're ecstatic and want to tell him how you see a long and happy future with him. Talk like that will scare him away. He should be telling you how happy he is that you're finally exclusive. Again, it's all about receiving. When he tells you how happy he is that you're exclusive, smile and say, **"Thanks!"**

If a man brings up exclusivity in a general way, saying, "So what do you think about exclusivity?" You can reply, **"Hmmm, what do you think?"** Throw the question back to him. He needs to bring up how he feels first. Follow his lead.

CHAPTER 9

Rich Men Can Be Poor Lovers

A Wealthy Man Doesn't Always Equal Happiness

Lower your standards for material items and increase your standards for inner qualities, like morals, kindness, and how a man treats you.

Don't ignore bad qualities because his black American Express card blinds you. When you understand men, you'll realize that a rich man who lavishes gifts on you may not be in love with you.

There's nothing wrong with dating a billionaire or a millionaire or a wealthy man. But too often I talk to women who tell me their goal is to meet and marry a rich man. They want the guy with all the material things — the Porsche, the house in the Hamptons, the ski house in Vail. He sends fancy Venus ET Fleur roses at the drop of a hat, takes them to posh restaurants, and gifts them gems from Tiffany's.

Material gestures are lovely. In fact, romantic gifts are important, as I explain further down. But getting extravagant gifts and being with a wealthy man shouldn't be your primary goal. Qualities like character, how he treats you, and whether he's into you are much more critical.

Some women think that if they get a rich guy, their lives will be a golden fairy tale. But you can feel poor inside while dating or being married to a mega-rich man. Even if you end up with a rich man, he could be stingy with money, love, and time. Conversely, you can feel rich and loved by a man who isn't incredibly wealthy.

Even if a man is generous and buys you everything you want, if you aren't in love, will you be content? Will all the Birkin bags, domestic staff, and trips to St. Bart's keep you happy if you're in a loveless marriage?

If you want true love and a man who treats you well, focus on that first. If he ends up being über rich, that's a bonus.

Focusing On Finances Can Backfire

What if your rich beau loses his money? Will you stick by him? Fortunes come and go. Will you still be happy with him? Will you be able to live with him in sickness and in health, whether he's rich or poor? If you wouldn't want to live with him even in the bad times, rethink your choice of a man.

You could end up like Mandy, 36, a woman I know, who married Rick, 50, a billionaire, because she wanted to be a fancy high-society wife. When Rick got ill, the charity balls and jet-setting lifestyle ended. She was no longer the doyenne of their well-to-do social circle. Her new normal was changing catheters and attending doctor's appointments. You need to love a man to want to stay, in good times and in bad.

Also when you're after wealth, men can sense it. It turns

them off. Or they may use you, too. They may want to showcase you as a trophy. You'll be in a partnership but not a love merger. They may use you for a fun time, which is what happened to my 40-year-old client, Susan.

Susan refused to date anyone who didn't make six figures or live in the right ZIP code. She thought she hit the jackpot when she met Ed, a plastic surgeon, 43, on Match. Ed listed "separated" on his profile. When he met Susan, he told her his divorce was imminent. He wined and dined Susan with fancy restaurants, trips, and little blue boxes from Tiffany's. That all sounded exciting, but when Susan said Ed rarely made plans with her on Saturday nights, I realized something was off. One day, she mustered the courage to turn him down for everything but Saturday night and learned the truth. He confessed he was still in love with his wife and hoping to win her back. Susan found out he'd been spending Saturdays with his children and his wife. On Saturday afternoons, he was helping them with projects around the house. Then he took his wife and their children to dinner.

Susan was hurt and felt like Ed had been using her. But she contributed to this situation. She placed too much importance on Ed's financial success. Plus she ignored the fundamental Saturday night rule. (As we talked about in Chapter 4.)

If you want to be wealthy be what you want to attract.

Write a bestseller. Start that online business. This way, you're more likely to be mingling amid wealthy men who are a mirror for you. After earning your millions, you may realize that it's not enough. While the money is fantastic, what you want most is true love. You want someone there for you while you're sick or having a bad day. You want a man who loves and cherishes you, which is a beautiful thing.

Gifts Are A Barometer

Getting romantic gifts from a man is important and often a sign he's thinking of you romantically. But expensive doesn't necessarily mean better. This is an area where women are often confused. If a man pays your rent and takes you on expensive shopping trips and buys you high-priced gifts, you may think he's a keeper. He could be. But he could simply be interested in a practical arrangement. It might not be about love, but convenience. He may keep you in his life as a showpiece. He may want to control you. He may have no intention of a long-term future.

You may start falling for a guy who spends $1,000 on a gown for you for a charity gala. You feel special because it's the first time someone bought you a $1,000 dress. Be cautious. He may have a lot of money and want to impress his friends with his hot new girlfriend. The dress is part of his plan to see and be seen. He may want to parade you out at fancy parties and events. It may not be about true love or being in a special relationship. This man may want to keep the relationship surface level. He may not see you in his life long-term, or if he does, it will be an arrangement.

If you're okay with this, that's fine. But if you want true love and intimacy, realize it's not about how many expensive gifts you can get. A man who showers you with gifts and who is generous isn't a bad thing, but beware of settling for crumbs. Yes, even a rich man who buys you a dozen roses, a Cartier watch, and books a Michelin-rated restaurant on Valentine's Day can toss crumbs. If a man gives you expensive romantic gifts and then disappears for three weeks, that's a bad sign.

If he's an amazing man who also gives you pricey romantic gifts, that's wonderful. But judging a man based only on the extravagance of his gifts isn't smart. You want a man who integrates you into his life, who is with you on Saturday nights, someone who moves the relationship forward because he can't live without you. You want a man who loves and cherishes you.

Sometimes a man will give you an expensive gift that's not romantic. This is problematic, too. If you get an expensive but non-romantic gift, like a high-end appliance or expensive fishing rod for your birthday, that's not a good development. When men give non-romantic gifts on your birthday or Valentine's Day while dating, they aren't feeling it with you. Something's off about the dynamic.

An exception is if he gives you a romantic gift and a practical gift to go along with it. Or if the practical gift — like a fishing rod — is something he bought, for example, on a random day, so you and he can go fishing with his family. In that case, it's a good sign, because his aim is likely for you to get to know his family better. If it's a fishing rod or an appliance on your birthday — with nothing else — that's not a good sign.

You deserve romantic gifts on Valentine's Day, your birthday, and other occasions from a loving man who's courting you and in your life. A man in love who sees a future with you buys romantic gifts.

A romantic gift can be expensive, but it doesn't have to be. A handwritten poem, a box of chocolates or heart-shaped scones (handmade by him) are a good sign and indicate a man is thinking of you romantically.

The Bottom Line

When a rich man lavishes you with gifts, it doesn't mean the man is in love with you. If you're looking for true love, other things — like whether he's loving, consistently in your life, and moving your relationship forward — are more important.

Romantic gifts are also important in a loving romantic relationship. If those romantic gifts are extravagant, that's a bonus, but pricey doesn't necessarily mean you have a great guy.

Also remember that rich men don't always make the best husbands. They aren't necessarily going to be generous with their love, money, or time. They may lose their money, too, and then what will you do?

Likewise, some women may dream of being with a man

in a particular profession — such as a surgeon — or one with an appealing surface characteristic. But if you want true love and a man who treats you well, focus on those aspects first. If he ends up being über rich (or has other characteristics you've dreamed about), that's a bonus. Sometimes the fantasy in your head of what you think will make you happy isn't the thing that will make you happy at all.

Dream *Girl* Dialogue

If a man gives you anything, even if you don't like it, it's polite to smile and say, **"Thank you!"** You should be grateful for every present a man gives you. If you love the gift, don't go on and on about how you never got one like it before. Your man will wonder if you're special. If it's romantic but not your style, don't criticize it. That's rude. Be thankful. Men will stop giving you romantic gifts if you start critiquing their choices.

If it's a gift that's beyond incredible, you can elaborate and say, **"Wow, thank you — this is beautiful,"** or **"Wow, thank you — this is stunning!"** Or something similar, depending on what it is. Be thankful and happy, but again, make sure not to go on and on about how you never received something so lovely. Types of compliments to avoid: "This gift is the best gift I've ever received — no man has ever been this thoughtful," or "No man has ever spent this much money on me."

If on your birthday the only gift you receive from him is something practical, like an appliance or a fishing rod for you to use to fish with him, don't be a drama queen by angrily telling him off. All you need to say is, **"Thank you."** Not only is it polite to thank him, but truly be thankful. Because this non-romantic gift is giving you valuable intel, showing you how he feels about you. Then reevaluate the relationship because non-romantic gifts during courtship aren't the greatest sign.

SECTION TWO

Communication

CHAPTER 10

Men Want a Relationship That Flows

Communication Isn't What It's Cracked Up to Be

Don't treat a man like he's your therapist.

In the initial stages of dating, revealing too much — whether it's good or bad — kills the chase. By holding back, you can keep the spark alive longer and have a beautiful courtship.

Because women don't understand men, they often bare their souls to men early on. Revealing secrets or getting ultra-emotional may cause you to get close to him fast, but you'll connect in a casual, unhealthy way and start to lose your allure. Don't show a man a window into your soul so soon.

A new man is a stranger. He could be out of your life in a flash. That's the nature of dating. Men are in and out, and you never know for sure who you're going to click with until it sticks. Why share so much personal stuff with someone who could break your heart, or perhaps use it against you in the future?

Some women may feel like they need to share early on to see how a man responds to their secrets to know if they have a future. But sharing secrets and personal information with someone you barely know isn't a healthy way of relating. Nor will a man's response show you much about whether you have a future together. Most men will be polite and listen as you share something personal, but inside they may be thinking, *Wow, she sounds damaged.* Or, *This is TMI for a first date.*

You'll be able to see if there's an emotional connection as you slowly get to know one another through courtship, and the way he handles issues and events that come up during courtship.

Also, when you share deep details with a man too soon, he can get bored and may find someone more mysterious to be with. When you're an open book on the first date, he has less to look forward to on dates two, three, four, five, and beyond. Even that guy you started dating who seems like a great guy can pull back and leave you scratching your head.

In some ways, dating is like interviewing for a job, where you put your best foot forward in the beginning.

It can be tempting early on to bond with a guy by sharing everything — the good and the bad — about yourself. But what happens is that a woman starts as the dream girl and ends up as the, "I'm not so sure how I feel about her anymore" girl.

When a woman first meets a man she likes and feels a connection and a physical attraction, she often feels so good inside that she thinks nothing can possibly go wrong. He seems so sweet and understanding. But that may only be short-lived.

Sometimes women share too much with a man early on

because they want to get close to a man really fast. They want a loving relationship *pronto*. Who doesn't? When you like a man and are attracted to him, it's normal to want it all wrapped up right away. It doesn't work that way, however. You can't force him to be your boyfriend early on just because you like him. You have to let the courtship dance unfold. Women who don't have faith in the courtship process, or who aren't aware of how it works, will try to abbreviate the slow dance of courtship by getting too close to a man really fast.

You need to see if he's the right man for you, and you don't figure it out during bonding conversations that are like therapy sessions. You figure it out by watching how he responds to issues that come up during courtship and how he treats you during courtship. Plus, men can lie, making it seem as if he's the man for you, when he's really not. Bonding can feel good in the moment, it gets you close fast, but a man usually pulls back once he's gotten too much of a woman too soon. He needs to work for you.

Date smart and protect yourself. Not everyone you meet is going to be a good guy. In the first few months of dating, it can be hard to tell.

Plus, even good guys in long-term relationships would prefer to know less. They don't want a deep conversation that makes their "head hurt." A man I know said those two words in quotes many years ago, and it has stuck in my mind for at least two decades. He was laughing when he said it, but it was something that frustrated him, too. Long, intense, emotional conversations—even with women who turned him on — drove him nuts.

A man doesn't want to hear about problems you're having with friends or how devastated you were when your former fiancé broke off your engagement. He doesn't want to be involved in a soap opera.

Once you know you are with a good guy who is in love and serious about you, you can share more. But even then, don't turn a man into your therapist. Even in a serious relationship, you should find other ways to vent about your problems, instead of relying on your boyfriend to be your only sounding board.

Keep quiet on other matters, too, like dietary choices or exercise. When you talk too much about health, even in response to a man's questions about your special diet, it can work against you on a date. You may answer his questions about your diet, and in doing so give away too much information about a health problem. Also, when you talk too much about your food plan, a man can feel like you're judging him.

Whether it's your divorce, a family drama, a difficult boss, your diet, your health, or anything negative or sensitive, hold back. If you don't, he may say, "She has issues." This can feel unfair, because everyone has their issues, and he may even be the one who asked you about your issues. This is why you need to enforce your boundaries by holding back initially.

Even if it's a positive development — such as how you got a huge promotion at work — don't spend the entire date talking about how long you waited for this promotion.

Never bring up sexual topics with a man, either. If you do, he may get the wrong idea and think you're hoping to initiate a sexual encounter. You want to let the man guide the conversation and the topics. Good date topics early on include hobbies, general information about your families, what type of sports and movies you like. Steer clear of political debates. If a man gets too deep, hoping to delve into a topic you don't want to discuss, you can always nicely change the subject.

Be careful, too, when men say they're looking for more communication. Some men — either in real life or on their online dating profiles — will say that "communication" is a big part of what they're looking for in a mate. A man may have gone to couples counseling where this was discussed as an integral reason why his past relationship tanked. He might think talking about the importance of communication makes him look like a good guy. But you need to realize that men don't want communication to the degree they say they want it. They definitely don't want it to the extent most women want it.

What men want is a relationship to flow, without major relationship discussions or deep conversations about the problems going on in your life, his life, or your relationship. When you give men the "communication" they ask for, it works against you. Men may even say they want to be with a talkative woman who isn't afraid of baring her soul to him on a first date. But it's smart to be wary of what men say they like about women.

Even Nice Guys Pull Back

Sometimes a good guy comes on strong, and you may feel comfortable enough to bond and share intimate details, in the rush of romantic and sexual excitement. When he starts to pull away, you may not make the connection between oversharing and the fact that he's pulling back. As quickly as he pushed himself into your life, he's out of there. This is when a woman complains the man is a "jerk," or a "Jekyll and Hyde." But what's happening is that she didn't understand him.

Even nice guys don't want to be your therapist. Most emotionally healthy men want the easygoing woman. They want a break from their stressful lives.

Some women ask, "I'm *not* easygoing. Isn't it fake to act that way on dates?" This is a good question, but my answer is that if you're not easygoing, you should work hard on this aspect of your personality while dating, and in anticipation of a healthy long-term relationship or marriage. You should do all you can to become your higher self. Your dating life will go more smoothly if you do this, as will all aspects of your life.

Sarah, 43, from Kentucky told me she shared personal details often with dates because the men seemed so interested. Like many women, Sarah thought she was being rude if she didn't answer every question a man asked.

Sarah contacted me because a man she was dating, Trevor, told her they needed to "take a break." She met Trevor, 45, at a party. The conversation on their first date focused on the misery she suffered at the hands of her ex and the low period since the divorce. Sarah vented to Trevor about her ex, her troubled teen, her difficult boss, and her health problems. Sarah had anger toward her ex and started crying on her and Trevor's second date. "I didn't want to get too personal, but he kept asking questions," Sarah told me. "He wanted to know all about my divorce and seemed so caring and was a good listener."

As the dates progressed, Trevor shared about his own abandonment issues due to a father who left his mother when he was a toddler.

Trevor eventually told Sarah that they needed time apart to get over their issues. Sarah may not have been a match for Trevor in the long run. We'll never know. But because the dates were like therapy sessions, they never had a fighting chance. I told Sarah that the next time a man asks her questions about her past, she should give light answers. If a question is too personal, avoid answering it in depth. Deflect in a light-hearted way.

You don't want to feel like you revealed too much too quickly, waking up the next morning and feeling like you overexposed yourself to someone you barely know. This isn't to say you should be mute on your dates or in a relationship. Just be cautious.

Realize, too, that with some men, you're damned if you

talk and damned if you don't. You can't do anything right. These guys aren't your guys. These men complain you don't talk enough about your life, and then when you talk more, they push you away because you're boring them. Don't let these men get to you. You're on the right path.

Ex Talk Is As Bad As Sex Talk

Don't be the unhealthy person who vents about their ex early on. It drags the mood of the relationship down. Instead of it being about you and the guy, it's about you and your exes.

If a man asks about your ex, give a surface answer. Don't feel obligated to say much more than that. A man will judge you for talking negatively about your ex. Whether you like it or not, this is how it *really* is. If you talk about how your ex was lazy and mean, it will reflect badly on you. He'll wonder why you attract lazy and mean men. Or he'll think you were part of the problem. He might wonder why you stayed with such a man. He may think you'll talk about him negatively in the future.

David, 38, from London, told me that when a woman goes on and on about a problem with a prior relationship, he wonders if she's over the ex. "It can be annoying when a woman can't stop talking about her ex. If she's angry or acts like she hates him, my feeling is she's still in love with him."

Also be wary of a guy who vents too much about his ex. You aren't his therapist or a social worker. Plus, a healthy guy who is attracted to you wants to woo you on dates, not spend precious time complaining about his ex.

When you're getting close to someone, at some point he'll usually let you in on what's going on with his ex. He'll explain what happened in his past relationship, the drama or no drama going on currently, whether his ex is in his life due to their child/children, or whether he has nothing to do with her. He does this because you're getting close. He wants you to be part of his life. After a few dates, some ex talk is okay. But depending on how much and what he says, it could be a pink or red flag.

Don't Be Too Authentic

Women in serious relationships also need to be careful. Sometimes women in long-term relationships tell me, "He's my boyfriend, he should know about all the issues I'm going through."

The problem is that many women overshare. While a good boyfriend does care about your problems, he doesn't want to know every detail. Too much drama is a lot to put on one person. I'm not suggesting you pretend nothing bothers you. But don't fall apart at every little thing.

It's a much healthier way of dating and relating when you hold back. Dragging each other into the abyss gets you nowhere.

Most men—whether they're a first date or a serious boyfriend—can't and don't want to process too much heavy emotional talk. Even the man who loves you and would never leave you would be happier if you were less intense.

I tried to give this tip to my client Mai, 40, from Tokyo, but she told me it wasn't healthy to curb communication with her boyfriend, Sam, who was 50 years old. She thought that sharing her problems and helping him with his problems was "authentic" and "spiritual."

The thing is, her way—texting him, "How are you?" each morning, telling him about problems with her sick niece, reminding him to call his ailing mother, and telling him about all the day-to-day drama in her life—wasn't healthy. She told him they needed to communicate better and used this line with him more than once: "We need to talk."

When she checked in on him, he rarely responded to her texts, and when he did, he gave one-word answers. Mai told me her texts to Sam were intended to be loving. But I doubt he saw it that way. Men don't appreciate that type of attention. They feel smothered and want to run the other way.

Mai didn't follow my advice, telling me that holding back was fake. Eventually, they got into an explosive fight, where she called him ungrateful and rude. He called her controlling and obsessive, and it ended.

Mai was devastated over their breakup and hurt over the names Sam called her. She thought she was being a caring girlfriend, and she felt used and unappreciated.

Even though you may be a wonderful woman—a caring daughter, a devoted mother, a responsible employee—it doesn't mean you'll make a man happy. A loving woman with a heart of gold can come off crazy, controlling, or clingy if she can't hold in her anger or frustrations about life and the relationship, or if she can't rein in intense feelings for a man. Many women have great intentions, like Mai, but they turn off a man because of their strong emotions. Even if you're a fantastic person and care about a man and the world in general, if you don't understand him and respect the differences between men and women, you will lose every single time.

Introverts Have It Easier

Many women think men want to be around talkative women who entertain them and are the life of the party. They think they'd be more popular with men if they were more extroverted. But actually, you have a slight advantage in the dating arena if you're an introvert. Extroverted clients who like to be the center of attention and like to entertain their dates are at a disadvantage. They need to learn to be better listeners, be more mysterious, not interrupt their dates, and talk less.

While being outgoing might get you certain things, like a gig on the speaker circuit or head of the cheerleading team, it won't necessarily be the trait that gets you a great relationship.

Often when you talk too much, it's because you're trying too hard, and a man will pick up on it. When you hold back, it's more mysterious, and the right man thinks you're

Karenna Alexander

special.

If you're a big talker, rein it in. You might realize that you're oversharing in general with everyone, possibly boring them, and even turning people — men and women — off by revealing too much. If this sounds like you, get a handle on this aspect of your personality so you can date better and be a better girlfriend. Men get turned off when you talk at them. You don't want men to tune you out. You want them to be hanging on your every word.

Make sure to listen more than you talk. Being a good listener is an alluring quality. It's not all about you. In fact, when you make it less about you and are a good listener, a man wants to know all about you.

Some people ask, "Well, what if I'm dating a man who doesn't talk a lot?" What I've found is when a man likes you, even if he's a quiet man, he'll make conversation. He'll realize that if he doesn't it might ruin the date, and when a guy likes you a lot, and is attracted to you and wants to see you again, he'll pull himself out of his comfort zone and make conversation because he wants you to have fun on the date. He won't expect you to lead the conversation. The men that do expect you to entertain them either are bored and don't like you enough or they may simply be looking for a woman to court them. There are those men out there, but I wouldn't recommend continuing to date such a man, unless you're comfortable being in the pursuer role.

While on a date with a man who really likes you, there may be silences here and there. When this happens, don't feel like you have to fill them. You can simply smile and look around the room. Perhaps your date is taking in the scene, happy to be with you, trying to think of how he's going to ask you for a second date.

Even when you're not talking about something deep, heed the less-is-more mantra.

Listen to Maurice, 46, from Italy, who said, "When someone babbles on as if they're running out of time, and it feels as if they are dumping as much information on me as possible in the littlest time, I sense desperation and insecurity."

Questions Mr. Right Asks

Be wary of nosy men. On a first date, you may encounter a nosy man. A man who presses hard for personal details and gets angry if you don't answer is a bad news guy who doesn't warrant a second date. If he gets angry that you're trying to protect your boundaries, imagine what else he'll get upset about down the line.

In a relationship, a man may pry and demand details about your prior relationships. This can be confusing for women who don't recognize what men are all about.

You'd think a guy who insists that you reveal information about your past cares about you. But often, the opposite is true.

Men who are into you tread lightly around deeply personal details. They don't want to pressure you. They don't want to upset you and risk never seeing you again.

They're just happy to be with you. If he senses he's striking a nerve, a man will move on to a lighter topic.

The respectful man who sees you as a dream girl knows you're perfect for him. He doesn't drill you about your exes. You make him happy, and that's all that matters. For example, he might have gotten the sense or heard through friends you were getting over a breakup with a cheater. Your dream guy will spend time showing you how he'd never cheat. He wants to win you over, not vet you. When he feels the brand of love I'm talking about, he'll spend his energy trying to impress you.

My client Sascha, 50, from NYC, was dating a man named Max, 51, who got mad because she wouldn't discuss ex-boyfriends or her ex-husband. When she met Max at a speed dating event, he was charming. But on subsequent dates, Sascha noticed he had a mean streak. He'd had an explosive divorce and contentious relationship with his ex, and he asked Sascha if she had similar horror stories. She didn't. Sascha's ex was a good father and a good husband. Ultimately, she and her ex had fallen out of love because they married young. Max got angry with her several times, telling her she was holding back.

Max's inquiries weren't healthy or respectful. They felt more controlling than caring. Sascha eventually broke up with him when she saw his true colors.

When I interviewed married clients with adoring husbands, they said their husbands rarely, if ever, asked about their past. They were so intent on winning over these ladies, they didn't ask. They had no doubts and didn't need to know about their pasts. Some may have asked a question or two, but nothing deep.

Some women want to know when and if they should share more about a prior relationship. There's usually never a need early on and typically a man in love with you doesn't want to drill you about your past. Eventually, if your ex was an absentee father or an abusive, out-of-control rageaholic, you can share more, and it will become apparent to your new man as he involves himself in your life. Remember, dating isn't therapy. Neither is marriage. Even your husband doesn't want to hear you venting all the time about your jerky ex.

When you get more serious with a man, you can reveal more about your past and your personal life. But even then, there's no need to share every detail.

A good guy who is interested in you asks questions, but typically he asks light and fun questions. A good man doesn't pry and ask personal questions that are hurtful. Early on, he wants to get to know you, and if there's a lull in conversation on a first date, he wants to keep the conversation going. Especially on a first date and in the beginning stages of dating, while he's trying to win you over, a man who is attracted will keep trying to move the conversation along by talking and asking questions. He tries to make you laugh. He doesn't want you to be bored. He wants you to have fun on the date so that you go out with him again.

He wants to know about your job, what sports you play, what films you enjoy, what books you read. He may try to find out what your favorite breakfast food is so that he can make you breakfast in bed when you finally sleep over at his house. He may ask you where you want to travel next because he's dreaming of a trip together.

If you're walking past a jewelry store, he might ask if you like silver or gold jewelry because he knows your birthday is coming up, and he wants to know what type of jewelry to buy. He'll ask about your favorite restaurants.

He may ask about your family because he's curious about who is important to you and who is in your life. He wants to know what pets you own because he's wondering if your pets and his will get along with one another. If he's turned on by you and is a relationship-minded man, he's thinking this far ahead. Questions like this are fine to answer.

My client Marlo, 39, from Boston, shared a cute story that illustrates how men gather information. Marlo said on her eighth date with Tom, 33, she ordered chocolate cake with white frosting for dessert. Tom asked, "So is chocolate with white frosting your all-time favorite cake, or do you like another kind?"

She replied, "Yes, it's my favorite." Marlo said she forgot they had that conversation. But she then remembered it when Tom took her away for her birthday weekend to a fancy spa in the Berkshires. He had their server bring out a chocolate cake with white frosting, ablaze with candles. That's when she realized why he'd been asking about her favorite cake. Back on the eighth date, he knew she was *the one*. He was gathering information because he wanted to make her birthday special. Besides the cake and the weekend away, Tom bought her diamond earrings. The pear-shaped engagement ring came three months later.

A good man who likes you will behave like Tom. He'll want to learn things about you so he can impress you on the next date and beyond. He'll ask questions to find out what's important to you so he can use that information to woo you.

Healthy Men Like Happy Women

A man wants to feel like he can make you happy. If you're sad and unhappy all the time, it's a drag. He feels like he's let you down. Even if he hasn't let you down, he feels responsible for your misery. He's happy with you and wonders why you can't be happy, too. Even if a man is attracted to you, your negative attitude can eventually repel him.

If you want to get a healthy man and keep him, you need to be your best self. Men love emotionally healthy women. They also like women who keep their cool and don't get ruffled easily. This may be something you need to cultivate if it's not second nature. Work on these things if you want to find a great guy.

Without the inner game, you'll be struggling to find a man. A quality man wants to be on a date with someone who gives him respite from his problems at work, his unhappy ex, or his crazy family. Because of you, Saturday nights become the most fun he's had all week.

If you want to be your higher self, and be happy in life

in general and in your relationship, work on this aspect of your personality with men you're dating, with a man you're in serious relationships with (i.e. engaged or married to), and with everyone else.

The happier you are, the more content your man will be and the happier your relationship will be. You should essentially be your higher self all the time.

Some women tell me, "Wow, this is just too much work." But you should realize it's also a lot of work and anguish to get back on the dating scene after a man has ghosted you because you were just too intense or your personality was too dark. Plus, when you start working on your insides slowly and you're seeing a man only once a week in the beginning, you have time to practice becoming your higher self. Practice makes perfect. This is when going to the spiritual gym, where you nourish your insides, comes in very handy. (See Chapter 19 for more.)

The Bottom Line

Be careful what you share with men. Dates aren't therapy sessions. Even if sharing deep secrets about your past gets you close to a man, it won't get you closer in the romantic sense.

Hot and heavy relationships that start quickly, with a woman bonding and sharing everything with a man, may appear picture-perfect and exciting on the outside, but they aren't necessarily healthy love matches.

Be careful, too, when a man presses for details. There's no need to answer every question he asks, especially if it feels too personal.

Even elaborating too much about the little things can drive a man up the wall. Sharing less also keeps the spark alive and makes you more mysterious to a man, and this will give you a beautiful romantic courtship.

Dream *Girl* Dialogue

Here's how to respond to questions from men on dates and how much to reveal to a man you're dating.

In the early stages of dating, say, **"I had a good day,"** when a man asks how your day went. This is a great answer, even if your ex finally picked up the last of his belongings from your home and you're a tad sad.

Early on in the dating process especially, nothing needs to be said about something so personal in your life. And on some level — despite the ex drama — you did have a good day, because everything else went fine. And the end of a marriage — while not the best feeling — is likely a good thing because it wasn't working and now you can find someone better for you.

If, while on a date, a man asks why your marriage ended (or why your last relationship ended), you can say, **"We're no longer together. We got divorced."** Because that's the truth. There's no need to act upset or tell him your ex cheated. Some women may get flustered and upset and look like they're about to cry, saying, "I can't talk about that. It's too upsetting." You're human, and it's normal to be upset, especially if the breakup is fresh. But if you don't hold back, you can lose your dream girl status.

Say, for example, that you work in the fashion industry and you just filed an HR complaint against your boss who is sexually harassing you. If a man on a first date asks how work is going, be cautious. You may be dying to talk about the issue at work because it's all you can think about. But besides the fact that it may not be in your best interest legally to speak to a stranger about a potential lawsuit, it's too heavy for a first date.

Instead, you can say, **"I had an interesting day today,"** or **"Work is always eventful."** If he keeps asking about your work, say something like, **"Every day in fashion is different. Like today, we got this great new line of skirts in from this hot new designer."** If he's pressing you about your job, it's better to talk about skirts instead of an emotionally devastating problem you're dealing with at work.

Sometimes a man will ask a personal question that throws you for a loop, such as, "How long has it been since you've been in love?" You can say, **"Hmmm, what a question."** Hopefully, he drops such a personal line of questioning. But if the man keeps pushing, you can reply, **"I don't feel comfortable answering that."** Most men won't persist if they sense you're uncomfortable, but it's good to have scripts ready so you don't get rattled on dates.

If a man asks you—while on a date or on the phone— why you're so quiet, just giggle. If you feel you need to say something, say, **"Hmmm, I guess I'm not a huge talker."** (Even if you are usually a big talker or had been very talkative on dates, you're no longer going to be a big talker on dates when following this advice, so this is an honest statement.) Usually guys who like you don't notice or don't pick on you for being on the quiet side. You can use a similar script if he asks why you don't text or call him enough: **"I'm not a big texter/caller."** Most men who like you will appreciate that. Many have the opposite problem and are bombarded by women who text or call too much.

When you're on a dinner date and a man wonders why you're ordering something bland, you can say, **"I like this type of food."** This is true. You like it because if you don't eat this type of food, you'll be sick, which is something you don't like. But don't tell him these foods make you sick. It's none of his business early on what illnesses or food sensitivities you have. Hold back—for as long as you can— about dietary restrictions due to health problems.

If a date is pushing you to "Have just one piece of pie," smile and say, **"No thanks, I don't like pie."**

If a man pushes another type of dessert on you, and you can't eat sugar due to a health constraint, you can respond by smiling and saying, **"No thanks. I'm soooo full after that great meal."**

Another thing that happens on a date is a man will ask you to have a drink or several drinks with him. If you're not a drinker, simply say, **"No thanks, I don't want one."** He may look puzzled, and ask, "Don't you drink?" You can nicely reply, **"I'm not a big drinker."** He may ask, "Why not have just one?" You can reply, **"No thanks, I'm good,"** or **"No thanks, I'm not in the mood today."**

One last tip on this subject: If a man ventures into any personal topic you don't want to discuss, nicely change the subject. Or if he continues to press you, say, **"I'm not comfortable talking about that right now."**

CHAPTER 11

Less is More Online

Think Short and Sweet in Online Encounters

Don't overshare online.

Your online dating profile should have the basics, like hobbies, favorite restaurants, and movies. You should include dealbreakers like age and locale, whether you smoke, and religion or lack thereof. You want to include enough to get a conversation started. But don't get too deep.

Keep your profile short and sweet. And don't give a detailed list of what you're looking for in a man. I realize these issues are important to you, and you're hoping to weed out bad news guys by laying it all out there. But too much too soon isn't good, especially to strangers perusing profiles online. Also, don't write about what you *don't* want. When you say, "I want someone who isn't mean to children, who doesn't play games, and who wants to have intimacy," you're revealing more than you realize. You come across as someone who has had bad experiences in the past with men who were mean to your children, who played games, and who didn't want intimacy.

The best way to keep bad news guys from coming into your life is to evaluate their character while following the strategies in this book.

You should be brimming with positivity and good vibes

in your online profile. When your online dating profile is negative, the men and the experiences you attract will be negative, too. Avoid making fun of yourself or looking down on yourself in any way, shape, or form.

Online dating photos are where you should make the most effort. But even in this area, you'll find that less is more. Two to three photographs are enough. Put up a headshot and one or two body shots. A man will be suspicious that you're hiding something if you don't post at least one full body shot. (Yes, you should be mysterious, but you do need one full body shot. It's only fair that a man sees your entire body.) Don't put up a photo gallery online of you and your pets and vacation spots, your friends and family members. It looks like you're trying too hard. It also kills the mystery.

The only time you will have to put up more than three photos is when you're on certain sites or apps that require you to include more than that amount. Some sites do require it, so you have no choice.

You may find yourself communicating with a man who asks for more photos. Move on from guys like this. Any guy who needs more than a headshot and body shot to date you isn't convinced you're his type. Or he's more serious about collecting photos of women than he is about dating you.

Another thing to remember while on a dating app is that you'll get peppered with questions. The best way to handle questions from online men is to answer in fewer words than them. And make sure to never get into a pen-pal situation with an online guy. After four text or email exchanges, cut a guy off. (This guideline is from the authors of *The Rules*, and I've found it works extremely well for my clients.) In fact, guys from apps who are very interested in you often ask for your number or a date in the first or second email or text because they don't want to risk not hearing from you again.

The men who keep chatting and never ask you out aren't looking to pin you down for a date. They're wasting your time.

You'll notice that if you stop chatting after four exchanges, a man may double text and ask you out. This happened to my client Heather, 38, who said she'd gotten to four exchanges with a guy on Tinder, and he kept texting, asking about her day. But he hadn't asked her out. She loved his profile and wanted to know what to do. "Stop texting him!" I advised. He asked her out the next day, and they went out for drinks the next week.

Other times, men drop off if you don't text much, but that's okay. This saves you time, weeding out men who aren't that interested in connecting with you in person.

If you help a guy along—asking him questions and making it convenient for him to ask you out by hinting about your interest or availability—you never know if he was going to ask you out on his own. He may only be on the date with you because you gave him a push.

Social Media Mystique

Just like in real life and online dating sites, you should have a less-is-more approach with your social media accounts. It's best to be cautious when involving a man in your social media life, because if you don't, you can lose your mystique.

Let men you've met in real life or on a dating site friend request you first on Facebook and approach you first on other social media sites. Even better, don't accept a friend request from a man on Facebook, and if he follows you on Twitter, Instagram, or other sites, don't follow him back. Barely acknowledge he exists there. Sometimes when a woman delays accepting a social media request from a prospective love interest, the guy forgets about it.

It's best to hold off from accepting a social media request from a man you're dating because it makes things more complicated while you're dating and if you break up. Plus, when you're part of a man's social media circle, you're more aware of what he's doing when you're not together. This is never a good thing for your head.

If you're on social media constantly or if you work together or have friends in common, it might be too awkward to ignore a man's social media request. You may have to accept it, but try to delay as long as possible, and even if you do add a man to your social media circle, it's best to interact with him as little as possible there.

Also, post only a few highlights on your social profiles. Be as classy as possible, and try not to live your life on social media. This should be how you act anyhow, whether your love interest is in your social media universe or not.

Of course, just like you don't initiate anything with a man in real life, don't make overtures to any man on social media sites. It comes across as desperate and pushy when you insert yourself in a man's social media life right away.

And never post a photo of you and the man you're dating on your social media sites. If he wants to photograph the two of you and post it, that's fine. He can broadcast you to the world, but if you do so, you look desperate. And never check social media while on dates. For the most part, taking out your phone on a date is rude. All daters — men and women — complain about this. Leave your phone in your handbag.

The Bottom Line

Less is more online. Just like in real life. (As you will recall from Chapter 6.) Nothing good will come out of a lengthy online dating profile. Long profiles are unnecessary, boring, and can be a big turnoff, especially if you include anything negative. The shorter and sweeter your profile and the fewer photos you post, the more mysterious you are to a man. When on an app or website, cut a man off after four texts or emails. You never want to be a pen pal with someone you have never met. The less-is-more approach goes for social media sites, too. You can ruin the mystery if you reveal too much information on Facebook, Instagram, Twitter, and other social sites.

Dream *Girl* Dialogue

Here's a short description that works on an online dating site, like Tinder: **"I'm a mixed-media artist who likes** modern art museums and NYC. I'm also a film buff who enjoys spy dramas like Homeland and Jack Ryan. Love to play tennis and travel. Long Island-based."

Here's an example of a bad Tinder description and then the revised version that is more appealing.

> **Bad Tinder Example:**
> *Still single at 32, just like that hot mess Bridget Jones, hoping to take a stab at online dating in case my Mr. Darcy shows up.*

> **Improved Tinder Example:**
> **Chicago-based Renée Zellweger look-alike who plays pickleball, works out, and travels. I'm a lover of spy novels, and The Matrix is my all-time favorite movie.**

While the Bad Tinder Example is witty, it puts her down. The Improved Tinder Example is physically descriptive and lists basic fun and light information that isn't too deep.

Below is a script of a successful online dating exchange that gets the job done. My client dated this man, and he turned out to be a serious boyfriend. As you'll see, she paces the conversation by not replying on weekends and not replying too quickly. She also wrote less than him and let him take the lead.

> **HIM (Friday 3 p.m.)**
> *Hi there. I liked your profile. You're pretty and smart. I also like going to Broadway shows, and when I was a kid, I had a small role in an off-*

Broadway production. I'll have to tell you about it sometime. Maybe we can meet up, and I can tell you the story. Would you prefer to talk or just meet up?

HER (Monday noon)
Hi, thanks. Cool about Broadway! Talking sounds good.

HIM (Monday 2 p.m.)
Here's my cell number: xxx-xxx-xxxx

HER (Monday 5 p.m.)
Here's mine: xxx-xxx-xxxx

In the above scenario, the man moved it offline quickly. In his first message, he asks to meet up. (One thing to note is that online dating scammers tend to want to move offline quickly, but in this scenario, she got a good vibe from the man. He gave no signs of being a scammer.) He also mentions that he read her profile, which is a good sign he's interested in her, unlike some men who email or text many women the same form letter. They do this blindly, hoping to get as many bites as possible.

CHAPTER 12

Nagging Gets You Nowhere

A Man Doesn't Change That Easily

Don't nag or try to change a man.

Men don't change easily. Plus, nagging and trying to change a man are emasculating behaviors that remind men of mothers or bosses. It's not romantic, whether you're on a first date or with a serious boyfriend (or a husband).

It's also a waste of energy. If you want a beautiful courtship that runs smoothly, you need to understand this crucial characteristic about men.

Be his girlfriend, not his guru.

A man may know he needs to change, but he doesn't want to hear it from you. It comes across as controlling. It makes him feel worse about himself, and your critique is a reflection of your maturity and your level of happiness.

A man wants to be with someone soft and easygoing who accepts him as he is. He won't be dreaming about the date all week if he knows you're going to be picking on him for something he's said or done. He wants to be with someone who trusts and respects him and his choices—a woman who knows he would never cheat, so she lets him do what he wants, and she would never think of checking up on him, demanding to know why he doesn't call her more or do more for her.

A man doesn't want to be told how he needs to treat you better. Neither does he want to be nagged about his health, his relationship with his family, how he conducts himself at work, how he dresses, or how he interacts with his friends.

A man hates when you send super long texts about a problem you have with him. He'll most likely be rolling his eyes as the text comes in. He may share it with friends or co-workers — when a man gets a text like this, he needs to vent. If you nag him in person, he may not roll his eyes in front of you, but he'll hate it.

One reason many men lose sexual interest in their mates is because women nag and don't accept their man for who he is. A cool, confident, and happy woman isn't picking at or trying to change her man. She's mature enough to realize that no man is perfect and no man will solve all her problems, and she accepts the good and overlooks the bad. Go with the flow, and he'll think you're special.

There are exceptions, and a woman shouldn't ignore big things, like cheating or unsafe behavior, but she overlooks the small stuff. If something is so bad that you want to constantly nag your man about it, re-think whether he's the one for you.

There are times you may need to address issues that come up — for example, if a man is clueless about courtship because he's spoiled or hasn't dated a lot or if he hasn't proposed in one year. (Details on these issues in Chapters 1, 4, and 22.) But in general, work on acceptance and being grateful for what you have. Even though it can be hard to hold your tongue at times, it's harder to be in a relationship that started great but turned sour because you nagged and complained too much.

Which would you rather have: a romantic relationship with your boyfriend who always wants to be with you or a man who prefers to hang out on weekends with the guys? That's what happens when you nag too much. Boyfriends skip Saturday nights to play hockey with the guys, or they delay proposing or may never propose. They may break up with you and start dating someone else.

I overheard Roth, a 50-something musician from Vermont, having a conversation about dating. When a woman said, "Men just want to be left alone," Roth disagreed. "No, we don't want to be left alone," Roth said. "But we want to be appreciated for who we are, and we want space. When the right woman gives you that, we won't cheat."

When you—beautiful you—are easy to be with, a man wants to be with you all the time.

Too many women today are trying to change the man they're dating. They like the guy but want him to be nicer, richer, smarter, a better dresser. They nag and criticize, thinking that will get them somewhere. It never does.

Alternately, some women act insecure around their boyfriends, pestering them for not being caring or loving enough. Or they show jealousy. Jackson, 39, from Australia, said he broke up with his latest girlfriend because she was jealous and created drama. "When I'd get a notification on my iPhone, even if it was from a weather channel, she'd look at me suspiciously and then ask me whether it was another woman texting me. She was always harping on something," Jackson said.

If you aren't happy with the man you're with, find a different one who has what you want. Don't criticize the one you have because it will harm the relationship and you won't be happy anyhow.

Think about how you feel when someone tries to change you. From the backseat driver who tells you how to drive better to the well-meaning friend who thinks you would look better 10 pounds thinner, do you want to hear it? You probably already know how you should drive and that you'd look better thinner. Hearing it from someone else doesn't get you any closer to changing.

Let The Small Stuff Go

Instead of trying to change your boyfriend or offering unsolicited advice, learn strategies to let go. Holding back isn't always easy. The urge to nag is powerful, especially if you think you're right and feel as if you're helping.

If you're struggling with this, you may need to do some work in the spiritual gym. (See Chapter 19 for more on this.)

A Hong Kong-based client named Lisa, 40, was telling me how she repeatedly told her boyfriend, Mack, 40, that he was too passive when asking for promotions or raises. She wanted to help him become more successful in his career and was critical of what she perceived as lack of ambition. She even compared him to another guy. She complained to me that they weren't getting along and that he was acting distant. She couldn't understand why he wasn't taking her "fantastic" advice.

During our consultation, Lisa realized how controlling and rude she was being. Meanwhile, she was struggling at her own job and had other personal issues, which she needed to make a priority. She was ignoring her life and wasting energy nagging her boyfriend who didn't want the help. He eventually did ask for a raise, but he did it on his own time, after consulting a mentor at work.

Lisa realized she was taking the wrong approach and worked hard on this aspect of her personality. Whenever she felt like complaining or nagging her boyfriend, she vented to me. She also worked hard at being grateful for his good qualities. He had many good qualities, but she was focusing on those she perceived as negative. When he finally proposed, they were getting along better than ever because she finally learned to love him as is.

One thing I had her do was make daily gratitude lists, focusing on the fact that he loved her to death and treated her like gold (especially when she wasn't nagging). They had fun together, and she realized he was the best boyfriend she'd ever dated. Even though he wasn't as ambitious as she would have liked, he was still smart and did well in his career. She started to see how damaging her nagging had been to the relationship, and she also realized she was looking for perfection.

Chances are that if you're controlling with men, you're controlling in other parts of life. So improving yourself in this aspect of your dating life will spill over into the rest of your life, and the relationships you have with others will be more fulfilling.

Being calm and collected in a relationship isn't easy. It can be hard, especially the longer you're involved with someone and the more you care about him and the relationship.

Some women start feeling entitled to be rude or act like a diva with a man once he's hooked on them. Some women — once they're more comfortable in the relationship — think their man will never leave once he's said "I love you" and introduced them to family and friends. Some men do and will put up with nagging while dating, in serious relationships, and marriages; yet while they put up with it, they hate it. It hardly ever works. They don't change. Or if they do, it often doesn't last, or they resent you for making them change.

Also, never belittle a man who is trying to impress you. For example, I know a woman who was hoping the man she was dating would send flowers to her workplace instead of her apartment. She wanted to showcase them to work colleagues. When an elaborate arrangement of two dozen red roses arrived at her house, she said, "Pretty flowers, but didn't you get the memo that you're supposed to send them to a lady's workplace?"

The man thought the arrangement was going to thrill her, and once she made that comment, he pulled back and stopped calling. Who can blame him? He was trying to impress her, not her colleagues, and she wasn't grateful.

A man might not leave after one biting remark. But he

may take longer to propose. Even if you stay together, why would you want to drag the mood of your relationship down? Be your higher self as often as you can, and your relationship will be better for it.

Issues will come up. When engaged and married, there will be disagreements about your living situation, money, family, and more. If you aren't working on improving any dark sides of your personality right now, you should be. Excessive nagging and complaining will put a damper on your relationship with him, and it will affect the quality of your future relationship. Surrendering can be difficult, but when women master having a positive vibe and a great mindset, courtships and relationships are happier.

Instead Of Lashing Out, Hold Off

Never say anything in the heat of the moment. Control your anger.

Don't mention anything you're upset about unless you've thought it out and are calm, cool, and collected. Oftentimes, problems that can seem so big in the moment are issues you can let slide.

You can't take that mean comment back, but if an issue needs to be addressed, you can say something eventually when you're calmer and you've thought of the best possible way to say it. This way, you can avoid needless conflict.

(If he's asking for an immediate response, and you feel you can say it a non-heated and calm way, then feel free to respond.)

Another client, Natasha, 37, from Singapore, operated on this principle of holding back while dating a cute guy named Zack, 35, whom she liked a lot. Soon after they slept together, he started turning his back on her after sex.

She was a confident woman and had tons of men chasing her. Everything seemed to go well in this relationship for the first few months, and then the back turning started one night soon after they started sleeping together. She was upset and texted me in the bathroom. Maybe he's busy at work, she thought? Or maybe he never wanted anything serious? Maybe he wanted a good night's rest so he could get up early in the morning? Or maybe he wasn't feeling well that night?

She didn't know what was going on. This was in the early stages of their relationship, and the lack of intimacy bothered her. "I wanted to shake him awake and tell him how hurtful he was being," Natasha said.

I texted Natasha back, telling her to act like her cool self and pretend nothing was bothering her. She needed to wait it out. Acting like she wasn't upset wasn't going to be easy, but her other options weren't that great, either. She could have woken him up and complained that he wasn't being affectionate, which was her first instinct. She could have started acting clingy. The next morning she could have given Zack the silent treatment. She could have asked him, "Is the sex *that* bad?"

She agreed none of these options were that great, and she said she wasn't ready to break up with him. Also, she wasn't sure if she was blowing his back turning out of proportion.

She knew that if she had a talk, she wasn't going to change him. By saying nothing, she could keep her self-esteem intact and have a fun Sunday with him. They'd made plans to go to a new brunch place near his house and then go sailing on his boat.

To keep herself sane and content that night, Natasha went inside to the spiritual gym, filling her mind with beautiful, loving mantras. After a while, she barely noticed his lack of affection because she filled up her insides so well. It did take a lot of restraint at first, plus inner work and a decision that she wanted to be her higher self in this situation.

She kept repeating a mantra similar to this one, which I adapted from Ellen Fein and Sherrie Schneider, to herself:

I'm the coolest girl he knows. He loves me. My father loves me. Everyone loves me. God loves me. (If you don't believe in God, you can use another spiritual being or higher power as a substitute.)

She worked herself up into feeling so cool and good about herself, his behavior didn't bother her quite as much. All this self-talk and inner work while lying in bed with him—back turned to her—helped.

"The next morning, he was sweet and happy and kissed me and asked if I needed anything at the store because he was running out to buy a few things," she said. "I'm certain that if I had gotten in a bad mood over his lack of affection, the morning would have been ruined. I'm glad I had a fun weekend with him and didn't act like an emotional wreck on Sunday. It would have ruined a perfectly fun day," said

Natasha.

Observe how a guy treats you on his own — without prodding — and then decide whether you can live with it.

You can try to force a man to do something in a relationship, and it might work short-term, but it won't be coming authentically from the guy, and it doesn't often work in the long run. Because Natasha wasn't sure Zack was the man for her, she continued to go on coffee and drink dates with other men the whole time she was dating Zack. (As we discussed in Chapter 8.)

The back turning continued and was one aspect of Zack's personality that didn't mesh with hers. She wanted more intimacy and romance. Other problems cropped up, and she knew she deserved better. She broke up with him but doesn't regret dating him because she learned strategies to be her higher self. While she wasn't able to change his lack of affection, she did change her attitude, and that made all the difference.

Even if you're with Mr. Right, he may do something at some point that's insensitive. When that happens, mirror Natasha's attitude.

Maybe your lover won't feel like having sex on a night you're dying to have sex. Maybe you're feeling insecure about your weight and you catch him looking at the skinny waitress serving cocktails on the beach. Or maybe he takes your sister's side in a family disagreement because he thinks she's being more reasonable. Or an old girlfriend calls, playing the damsel in distress; he may not want her back, but she annoys you because her pleas for help disrupt your time together.

In all these situations, let the negative feelings roll off your back.

No matter how great your boyfriend is, he won't fill all the holes inside of you. You need to do the inner work, like Natasha did.

The Bottom Line

Appreciate your man for who he is. Nagging a man doesn't work. It usually doesn't change him in the long run. In fact, it may drive him further away. If you're dating a man with an unbearable characteristic, it would be better to break up.

Sometimes letting things roll off your back is difficult, so you may need to do inner work. You must create your own fairy tale. Realize that no man is going to be your savior. You need to do the work to love yourself.

Even when you meet Mr. Right, you can't expect him to make you happy all of the time.

Dream *Girl* Dialogue

As I said, nothing needed to be said in the situation with the back turner in bed (or in many dating situations where you're feeling hurt or confused), except words to yourself, like the beautiful ones Natasha told herself. Here's another gorgeous mantra to say to yourself if you're in a similar frustrating situation:

"I'm a beautiful woman on the inside and outside, and I'll make a man incredibly happy someday. If this guy doesn't see what he's got, he's not on my level, and I don't want to be with him. There's always a new man around the corner."

Also, if a man insists that you respond in the moment to a question, when you're angry and fear that you'll lose your cool, here's a simple script to remember to use, **"Let me think about that and get back to you."**

CHAPTER 13

Don't Go Investigative Reporter on a Man

You Won't Get the Intel You Want

Don't interrogate a man on dates.

Even if you're on a date with a man who is smitten, you can sabotage by asking him too many questions. You become the one pushing the relationship forward. When you ask too many questions, you turn the balance of the relationship around. You get into masculine pursuer mode while the man becomes the receiver, which is more of a feminine role.

Quite simply, too many questions are a turnoff to a man. By asking questions you come across as nosy, prying, and controlling. You can appear desperate or as if you care too much, and this will kill the chase.

It's better to let your date guide the conversation like he does throughout courtship.

When you're with a guy who is head over heels, you'll notice you barely have to ask any questions at all because he keeps the conversation going and flowing.

Also, you can gather more information by listening than by talking and asking questions.

When you ask a man questions early on in a relationship,

you're also revealing more than you think. Depending on what and how many questions you ask, you risk losing your mystique. Whatever you question him about is what he thinks you're focused on. Anything personal you ask gets magnified in his mind.

For example, when you ask a man, "Do you want children?" he's automatically thinking, *She wants children with me.* When you ask him how well his business fared during the COVID pandemic, he may wonder if he's being judged. He may think, *Is she asking because she wants to know if I can be a good provider?* Or if you ask, "Do your kids live with you or your wife most of the time?" he may wonder, *Hmmmm, she's thinking too far in advance about how my custody situation might affect her.*

You kill the chase with intrusive questions. If it's just a first date, he may think you're taking this encounter way too seriously. A healthy normal guy will run the other way when you come on too strong by asking too many questions. Even innocuous questions can make a guy feel you're interrogating him. Often women ask questions to be polite. They may not even be that curious, but men often take questioning the wrong way.

Some women think if they come to the first few dates armed with questions, they're being smart and proactive. They tell me they're asking questions to vet a man. They want him to answer certain key questions, either on a first date or in an email exchange before the first date. They think they're saving time. They're adamant that they don't have time to date a man who has a quality, like an addiction, that's a dealbreaker. They insist they should be able to ask him if he's a smoker or drug user or any other deal-breaker question.

Even if you question a man as an investigative reporter would, it doesn't mean he'll tell you the truth. He won't give you the scoop you want. A man will often tell you what you want to hear. You may waste more time in the long run by interrogating a guy. He could lie, and that will give you a false sense of security.

If you ask, for example, "Do you have a good relationship with your parents?" he may never tell you he hates his mother. But if you date the guy for a while, the truth will be revealed. It's hard for a man to hide something like that.

Some women who want kids vet men early on about whether they want them too. If you ask a man on a first date if he wants children, he could reply, "No, I hate kids and never want children." This would weed him out faster, sure. But you'll turn off many guys who do want children, so it's risky to ask. Even a man who says, "No, I don't want children," could change his mind. A guy may not be honest, either. He might not want kids but could say, "Yes I do," because he thinks you want children and he wants to keep dating you for a while.

I'm big into saving time, but asking probing questions — especially in the early dating stages — isn't the best way to do that. If you let him reveal himself on his timetable and watch his actions, you'll learn what you need to know.

Quinn, 39, from Miami, had a woman press him on their first date about whether he'd have more children. "Even if

I did want to have another kid, that isn't the time or the place to ask the question," he said. She was his physical type — a blonde lingerie model — but he couldn't get past the desperation and lack of mystery.

You're giving away all your power when you ask a question like this. Think of where the guy is coming from. He may or may not want children. But how can a guy tell you on a first date whether there's a chance he's going to have children with you? That's kind of what you're asking, right?

It would be great if you could vet a guy on the first date and have a relationship all wrapped up right away. But you need to let the courtship dance unfold slowly. The more you push a man to answer a personal question, the less likely he'll want to answer. The fewer questions you ask and the more you listen and are quiet and mysterious, the more he'll reveal.

Many women think nothing of asking a guy what he does for a living. They're career-oriented and love talking about their job and figure a man would as well, so they pepper him with questions. But often when you ask a guy about his job, he wonders in the back of his mind if you're inquiring to see if he's a high earner. He may think to himself, *Whoa, hold up. We just met and you want to know if I can support you and a family?* Let him volunteer what he does for a living, and let him share, on his own timetable, details about his career.

I once overheard a woman on a date at a bar ask a man if there were opportunities for him to move up at his company. She barely knew him and seemed concerned about his future, and he looked uncomfortable and cut the conversation short.

Straight From The Horse's Mouth

Mario, 43, said he'd been on many dates through online dating apps. When I asked him the biggest complaint he had on initial dates with women, he said, "I don't want to be interviewed. My work life is stressful enough. I feel like a lot of women are interviewing me about deeply personal things. They need to chill."

Dozens of men said that women ask questions that are too deep so early on. Questions like:

- Do you want to get married again?
- Why did your last relationship end?
- Is your job secure?
- Do you think your family will like me?
- Did you ever think of going for a manager's position instead of just being an employee?
- Are your parents happily married?
- How often do you talk to your mom?
- Do you have a good relationship with your children?
- Do you do drugs?

Eventually, you can ask personal questions. But do so in a sparing way and only in certain situations. Hopefully, he volunteers answers to important personal questions. But if he doesn't, don't worry — there's a time and a way to ask.

How And When To Ask Questions

In the beginning there's no need to ask serious questions. But eventually, as a relationship progresses to a more serious level, it may be helpful to do so, depending on the circumstances. There may be other sensitive topics to bring up eventually, too, if he doesn't bring them up.

When you ask these questions, you have to stress actions over words, so take his responses with a grain of salt. But sometimes asking questions can be helpful. In one scenario, a client named Melodie, from China, was with a man who would bring up his ex often on dates. She started to think perhaps it was a red flag. I decided to have her ask a few questions that I was hoping would put her mind at ease. This was six months in, and she was hoping there was a future. He was doing all the right things, moving things forward, seeing her on Saturday nights, and talking about a future. The only thing that nagged at her was the fact that he seemed to bring up the ex a lot.

I told her that the next time he brought up his ex, she should casually ask him why their relationship ended. And after he answers, she could just as casually ask how they met.

You'll often find out through conversations from him and others, and through observations, as to why they broke up. If it's never revealed what happened with his ex, you can ask. You want to know how it ended because if she broke up with him and he's devastated, he might still carry a torch. If it didn't work because they fell out of love, then there's probably no threat.

Also, it's important to find out how they met. If it started passionately, with him chasing her and her breaking up with him, you want to know this. If the ending of that relationship was devastating to him, he could still be in love with her. If she was the pursuer and it ended because they fell out of love, this is also good to know. It's easier for a man to walk away from that type of relationship.

When Melodie asked, he told her he and his ex were always friends but not lovers, and they married because she got pregnant and they wanted to stay together for their child. Melodie felt much better when she realized that he was never truly in love with his ex. He was only bringing her up because he wanted Melodie to know that she was still in his life because they had a child together. He proposed to Melodie five months later, but before doing so, he explained that he brought up his ex many times, hoping to start a conversation about some of the problems she caused in his life. But he always stopped himself because he didn't want to scare Melodie away.

The Bottom Line

If you want to keep the spark alive and have a beautiful

courtship, refrain from asking a man too many questions. The less nosy you appear, the more alluring and mysterious you are to a man. Men hate being interrogated, and even the most innocuous questions can work against you. In fact, early on you barely have to ask any questions at all of an interested man.

There are times you may have to ask more personal questions eventually, but it's not necessary to ask early on. Plus, keep in mind that even when a guy gives you personal information, it's through his lens. There's always another side to the story. Consider everything, including his actions and your observations about situations.

Dream *Girl* Dialogue

Here are examples of how to ask questions while on a date.

A man may say something like, "You're quiet, do you have any questions for me?" Ask something lighthearted, such as, **"Seen any good movies lately?"** or **"What type of sports do you play?"** or **"What are your hobbies?"**

No need to get deep on a first date or even beyond. Sometimes you can ask questions back. Like if he asks, "What movies do you like?" you can respond by saying, **"I like indie movies. What about you?"**

However, if in the early stages of dating, he asks something serious or personal like, "What happened with your engagement?" don't respond in kind. You can answer the question in a surface way, saying, **"We didn't end up getting married."** But leave out, "What about you?"

If he's asking this same question six months in, this could be your chance—if he hasn't already told you—to find out what happened in his prior relationship. So after replying, you can ask, **"What about you?"**

In Melodie's case, she brought it up during dessert one Saturday night, after her boyfriend brought up his ex and his child. She casually asked, **"So why did you end up breaking up?"** After he explained, she lightly asked, **"How did you meet?"**

CHAPTER 14

Men Hate Compliments

Compliments Flatter Him But Don't Bring You Closer

Never compliment a man.

Men should be complimenting you during courtship. When you truly understand men, you'll see that compliments from you kill the chase and dim the spark.

While you can certainly compliment a man for his looks, his ambition, his career, his temperament, and for a variety of other things, it won't win him over the way you want. Many women think if they compliment a man they're dating, they'll bond with him. Even if you bond, you won't get closer to him, not in the dream girl sense. The relationship will become casual quickly. You're no longer a mystery, and the fun starts to fizzle.

Compliments might flatter him and cause him to like you for the compliments and for the ego boost, but compliments won't get you to become his dream girl or remain his dream girl. He'll feel as if he's conquered you. You may get closer and get to know one another better through sharing compliments, and he may even think of you as a sweet girl who is nice to be around—but he won't get the same thrill he would get from a woman who is more elusive.

This advice may sound mean on the surface. But you need to realize that compliments are like saying "I love you" to a man. Men read more into compliments than you intend. Masculine men start to feel uncomfortable when their dream girl compliments them. When you compliment a man, he blows it out of proportion, and it can scare him away.

When you give a guy you're dating compliments, it turns him into the prize. It turns the balance of the relationship upside down and you become the pursuer (masculine energy) while he becomes the receiver (feminine energy). A healthy masculine man wants to woo a woman by giving her compliments. A masculine man doesn't get mad at a woman for not lavishing compliments his way. In fact, he doesn't notice.

Beware of men who fish for compliments. Men who need compliments aren't great pursuers. They tend to want to be the prize, and they don't pursue or court women. You, of course, can have a relationship with one of them, but it gets topsy turvy when a man is expecting a woman to take on a masculine role.

One scenario I've seen occurs when a man either online or on a date says, "What did you like about my profile?" Be cautious and make a note that this man may not be a great pursuer.

If you're a nice, loving person, you'll likely be tempted to compliment a man. You may feel that a man appreciates compliments like you do. But men don't think like women.

If you think your relationship is fizzling and worry it's because you aren't complimenting him enough, don't worry. That's not the reason. In fact, the type of man who complains that you don't compliment him may be making excuses and finding problems because he's not quite that interested. Or he may be looking for an ego boost, not a real relationship.

Fishing for compliments can come from insecurity or egotism. Be wary of these types.

It's not that you don't think he's great. Of course you do. You wouldn't be dating him if you didn't. A man knows that if you're accepting dates, sleeping with him, spending time with him, meeting his family, and eventually taking yourself off the market for him, you like him and are attracted to him. Men have healthy egos, of course. But they're not fed by compliments or gifts or money from their dream girl. Women are the ones who flower in a relationship when complimented.

(When it comes to marriage, you don't need to be so strict in this area. You don't need to keep up the chase during marriage. You can build your husband up, once you've got him and are on one another's team, but even then you don't want to turn into the clingy girl who is always lavishing compliments on her husband. You want him to be complimenting you more.)

Be careful what a man says about compliments. If you ask a man if he likes compliments from a woman, he'll probably say, "Of course!" He likes the compliments because they stroke his ego.

I once saw an attractive woman at a bar compliment a man about how popular he was in high school and how much she had a crush on him. He glowed like a set of Roman candles in the sky on the Fourth of July. But that encounter didn't go anywhere. Even if it had, that compliment would likely have done more harm than good. When you compliment a guy, he realizes he's conquered you and doesn't try as hard.

Instead Of Compliments, Do This

The way to make a healthy man feel good is to be receptive to his pursuit, be happy and easygoing around him, and respect him. Don't nag or try to change or control him. Don't be mean or critical. Respect his decisions and accept him for who he is. When things don't go your way, don't pout.

Look hot on dates. Be easy to be with. If he picks a restaurant you aren't enamored by, be agreeable and happy because you're with him. Be grateful to be with a man you like who is courting you.

Those are the ways to make a man feel good. Not by complimenting him.

The Bottom Line

Compliments kill the chase. While compliments do flatter a man you're dating, they won't get you closer to him in a romantic sense. A healthy man in love who is courting a woman becomes uncomfortable with too many compliments from you. He may wonder if you're the mysterious catch he thought you were. He'll likely read more into compliments than what you intend, and this is when he's likely to pull back.

If you meet a man online or in real life who fishes for compliments, make a mental note that this man may not be a great pursuer down the road. Often, men fishing for compliments are looking to feed their egos and looking to be the prize in the relationship. A man should be giving you compliments during courtship.

Dream *Girl* Dialogue

A masculine man won't fish much for compliments. But if he does ask something like, "Do you think I'm cute?" You can give a short and sweet response, like, **"Sure!"** And giggle. Or better yet, just giggle.

What will be more likely to happen is a friend or relative will say, "He's cute, isn't he?" Say, **"Sure!"** and giggle. Or better yet, just giggle! (Even if your man isn't present for this conversation, your words could get back to him and it would work against you.)

If he gets a haircut or a new shirt and asks what you think of it, you can smile and say, **"It's nice!"**

Don't go overboard.

CHAPTER 15

It's Never That Complicated

If a Man is Into You, He'll Be in Your Life

Don't make excuses for a man who doesn't ask you out.

When a man likes you, you'll know. You won't be scratching your head, wondering. If you're confused about how he feels about you or he's making excuses due to his "complicated" life, it means he's not that interested in you. When a man doesn't make falling in love easy, it's usually a bad sign.

An interested man usually asks you out right away. He doesn't wait months or years to make the first move. When he isn't asking you out, there's a reason. It's usually not that he's too shy or confused. Or clueless. Or has too much baggage. Or is too busy. Or (fill in the blank). In a longer relationship, a man won't be confused about whether he sees a future with you.

Another excuse women make for men is, "He's playing games."

Some men may be cautious because they aren't sure how you feel about them (especially when you're following the courtship strategies in this book, which do keep men guessing). But a good guy in love wants to win you over, not jerk you around. An emotionally mature man who wants to woo you doesn't play games.

"My wife was the first woman I wanted to marry," said Jordan, 51, a CEO. "All I could think about was how I was going to make her mine. Playing games never entered my mind. She was special and different, and I didn't want to lose her."

When it seems like a guy is playing games, he's probably confused about how he feels about you, and when that happens, it means he's half in and half out. You want a man who's all in. If he is playing a game or if his life is so complicated that you can't be part of it, then he isn't the best catch anyhow.

There may be times when a man truly is too shy or too intimidated to ask you out, but be careful never to make an overture to that type of man.

What You See Is What You Get

If a man is too intimidated by your beauty, your looks, your stature, or wealth, that will surface in some way in your relationship. Same for if he's too busy, too shy, or too hurt over his last relationship to ask you out.

Say, for example, you think a guy is too proud to ask you out, so you ask him out. What will happen is that he'll be too proud to do other things, like propose to you. Plus, because you were the one asking him out, you'll never know if he *had* to have you. You'll never have the romantic courtship that's so essential to a fairy tale relationship and marriage. When you ask him out and push things along because you fear he's too shy or proud or intimidated, often what happens is that same issue pops up later in your relationship, causing problems.

If he's too busy to ask you out, he may *always* be too busy for you, even when you may need him dearly, like when you're stranded in a remote area with a flat tire or when you're sick in the hospital.

Are Men Really That Intimidated?

Women often make excuses that men are intimidated by them due to their job or their success or their beauty. A lot of times, that isn't the real reason.

Oftentimes men are scared because women are showing up in a masculine way in relationships. For example, it's intimidating to a man when a woman tries to control his behavior or demands that he talk more about his feelings. "We need to talk," is one of those phrases that make men want to run the other way. Another example is when a woman says, "We've been dating steadily for one month. I think you should take your online dating profile down, and we should be exclusive."

When a woman has masculine energy in a relationship, her relationships with men turn casual, and she doesn't feel loved or cherished.

I've seen men who were intimidated by a woman's success or beauty go after her anyway when they wanted to be with her badly enough. Some guys will better themselves while dating a woman they're interested in because they want to impress her. They turn into overachievers — or better versions of themselves — to win her over.

If a man wants you badly enough, he'll overcome obstacles to ask you out or to move the relationship forward.

For example, I know many shy guys who will go after a woman they want. I know a shy and awkward man — a friend of the family — who asked me for advice on how to approach a woman he liked. He got up the courage and called her to ask her out. It didn't work out because she wasn't interested, but he tried nonetheless because he was highly motivated to have a girlfriend, and he liked her.

There *are* times a man may be so intimidated by a woman that there is no way he can summon up the courage to ask her out. This can and does happen. But realize that if a man is too intimidated to ask you out because he feels like you're above him, he'll always be intimidated by you and that will show up throughout the relationship.

Saul, 53, from Germany, worked with a beautiful woman who was so gorgeous, he was afraid to ask her out. He tried a few times but could never do it. He dreamed about her and thought she was stunning, but he could never get up the courage to say more than a few words to her. Once at a work event, he had to leave early because he was so upset that she was sitting next to and laughing with another male co-worker. He gave up because he didn't think he was worthy of speaking to her.

The fact that he couldn't function around her didn't bode

well. If a man is too intimidated by your beauty to ask you out, that will always be an issue. Even if you ask him out, it won't work out the way you want. He may fall in love with your plain nanny because he feels content around her. He may feel uncomfortable around you and not good enough for you, and it won't be a match. He may feel insecure, and to make himself feel better he'll insult you.

Plus, that intimidated guy who couldn't make the first move by asking you out also won't be able to get through all the courtship hoops. You'll be the masculine one in the relationship, driving it forward because he's too intimidated.

Avoid Men Who Hint

One confusing thing that happens to single women is some men flirt, yet they don't have any intention of asking a woman out. Don't get distracted by cute guys who do this. They'll waste your time. Some women who agree with the principle to never ask out a guy think still it's okay to help him along or give hints. But hints are beneath you and obvious to a man.

For example, if you're at a party where you're talking to a man who tells you he wants to learn to play tennis, you may think it's okay to offer to teach him to play the game. Even if you think he's adorable and sense chemistry between the two of you, don't do it. Men don't need your help to ask you out — not when they're interested, and you want an interested guy.

Also, there's no need to stare at a man to show you're interested. He'll think you're too intense.

Beware, too, of men who make half-baked overtures. They say things like, "You're pretty like my ex-wife," or "You seem like you would make a good girlfriend." A woman might think she needs to meet this type of man halfway. When a guy flirts but isn't asking you out, it's usually because he isn't fully into having a relationship with you. He may go along with it if you meet him halfway, but it's more out of boredom or something else than a desire to be with you.

Some women become confused by these men because they seem so nice and helpful. They may be your biggest supporter at work. They give you compliments via text or in person. They text you every morning. But they never ever ask you out. These guys will waste so much of your time while they're waiting for their Mrs. Right.

While some of these men may be flirting solely because they're bored, others may be hoping you take the bull by the horns and ask them out so they don't have to be responsible for anything to do with the relationship. They don't want to do the work, nor do they want to be invested in the relationship. They can blame you when you complain that the relationship doesn't progress. Because you took the initiative, they have an out and may say something like, "You're the one who kept asking me out. I never wanted anything serious."

Also, if a guy in your circle is charming every time you

speak with him, it could be because he's trying to win you over for a whole host of reasons that have nothing to do with him wanting to date or be in a serious relationship. He may be trying to get something from you. Perhaps he sees you as a potential client or someone who can get him a great job, or maybe he wants to date your friend or sister. Or, if you're a reporter, he could be trying to charm you because he wants you to write a flattering feature about him. Or, it could be because you remind him of his sister, and he enjoys talking to you and bantering. He could be an outgoing guy who is friendly to everyone. Or he could just be bored. Flirting kills a few hours of downtime while he's at work.

If a man isn't seeing you as a dream girl, he's not your guy. Move on to the one who loves you.

Baggage Isn't A Barrier

People have baggage, especially as they get older and have been through more life experiences. Of course, some custody issues are complicated. Divorces are complicated.

But when he's the right guy, that complication regarding custody or his troublesome job is compartmentalized. He can still ardently pursue. A man having problems in one area of his life—for example, with his job—won't want to ruin a relationship with an amazing woman. You keep him going. A drama-free dream girl is hard to resist. She's like gold to a guy who is stressed over a high-pressure job or one who is dealing with a toxic custody situation.

Say a man has five toddlers with three different exes — he will still do everything and anything to convince a woman that he's excited about being with her and his "baggage" is workable. (And of course, you should consider whether you can live with his baggage, too.)

His relationship with you may not move as fast as it does when a couple is in their 20s and unencumbered by children or other issues. When a man has complicated baggage — like a contentious custody situation or messy divorce — it may take longer to integrate you fully into his life, but it will happen. He won't ditch you for it, and he'll be figuring out ways to make you a part of his life. He won't want to lose you. And if he doesn't care enough to figure out how to integrate you into his life, he wasn't your guy and would have made a half-hearted husband, if it even made it to that point.

Some women have a myriad of excuses for a man with baggage. They're convinced he's pulling back because he's afraid he's going to make the same mistake he did with his ex. "He was burned and doesn't want to get burned again. I just need to convince him that I'm much more mature than his ex, and we can make this work," they may say.

Instead, the guy in the above situation with baggage should be convincing you, "I know I just got divorced and things got messy with my ex, but I learned so much and am going to make my next relationship work."

Unrequited relationships are the biggest time killers ever. They can be tortuous. It's better to move on fast than to make excuses. By moving on, you'll start feeling better. It will take some time, but a successful relationship will happen if you keep at it.

If It Doesn't Flow, Let It Go

Going back to an old boyfriend usually doesn't work. Or even going back to someone you briefly dated or to someone online who tentatively made plans but never asked you out. When a guy is unsure about you in the beginning, or when a relationship breaks up over a major problem, it's best to move on.

If a relationship was complicated and problematic the first time you dated, chances are whatever got in the way the first time will get in the way again. That man's flaw doesn't usually disappear quickly. Also, a man who wasn't that interested in you initially won't all of a sudden become more ardent about you.

It can be tempting to go back to an ex, especially if you're lonely. A man who broke up with you might return a few months or a few years later and say, "I've changed. I am no longer a cheater, and I no longer lose my temper." But think carefully about taking back a guy who hurt you once. If he hurt you once, he can hurt you again. Once a man has done something, like cheat or abuse you, it's not smart to take him back because men don't change that easily that quickly, and you'll likely see that same behavior down the road.

It doesn't mean that a guy who broke up with you won't

stay with you or marry you. He might. But you'll always wonder, in the back of your mind, if he's going to break up with you again. Or do the thing (cheat, be abusive, or whatever it was) that caused the problem the first time.

If he left you the first time, you'll be insecure and secretly fear, "Is he going to leave me in the lurch when hard times hit?"

It's not that you aren't loyal. You should be with a man for richer, for poorer, in sickness and in health. But you want to be loyal to a good man who is also loyal, not to a man who hurt you once before. Men don't magically improve that easily.

It also doesn't work well when a single man you've known a long time — who has been in your orbit but has never pulled the trigger — asks you out. There's a good reason why he didn't ask you out before now.

My client Iris, 39, from Brooklyn, learned this the hard way. A cute man who looked familiar to her kept saying "hi" to her on OkCupid. She realized she'd gone to college with him, and he hung with the popular fraternity crowd back then. This guy, Brock, never asked her out in college.

He approached her frequently on OkCupid. She was flattered because she felt invisible to Brock in college. He sent her messages over the course of several months. But he never asked her out. At one point, Iris blocked him on OkCupid because she got so annoyed with the incessant messages that went nowhere. Then, a few weeks later, he was back, asking her out online. He must have created a new account because she'd blocked him under his old username. This time, he asked her to meet up, setting a firm day and place.

I advised her against going. But she'd just broken up with someone and said she needed to get out and meet other men to take her mind off her ex. I told her not to get her hopes up. She'd known Brock for years, and he'd never asked her out.

They planned to meet at a nice place near where they both lived. She walked in the rain, getting there a few minutes late. He wasn't there. She stuck around and eventually asked the bartender, "Did you see a tall guy with reddish hair come in? We were supposed to meet at 7:30." The bartender said he didn't notice anyone fitting that description come in that afternoon or evening. She ordered a Prosecco, kept checking her phone, thinking he would text her that he was running late or canceling. After 45 minutes, she left.

She never heard from him again. The experience with Brock strengthened her resolve to steer clear of a man who doesn't make the move to ask her out right away or fairly soon after meeting.

The Bottom Line

A man who is interested in you won't make things complicated. You won't be confused whether he's in or out. When you have to make excuses for a man, it means you're with the wrong man.

If you ask a man out because you fear that he's too shy

or proud or too "whatever," that same trait will always be there. If a guy isn't asking you on a first date or moving the relationship forward, there's a good reason. Heed the silence.

Also be leery of men who are in your orbit for a long time, but never pull the trigger and ask you out. Or exes who suddenly come back and say, "I've changed."

Dream *Girl* Dialogue

Here's how to respond when you're with an ambivalent man and how to respond when a man you like compliments you but does nothing else.

If a guy you're dating says, "I'm confused how I feel about you because I just got out of a complicated relationship," or says, "I'm going through a lot at work this month so I need to take a break, just for this month," there's not much to say except, **"Ok, no worries."** Then be on to the next date with a new guy.

If a guy who skips several months tries to come back into your life, think long and hard about letting him back in. This is where an individual consult with me to assess your exact situation would come in handy. But I have to say, I've rarely seen it work out well.

If a man flirts, giving you compliments, telling you how pretty you are, all you need to do is say, **"Thanks!"** No need to compliment him back (even if you think he's looking for a sign that you like him). And definitely don't ask him out. He doesn't need your help. If he doesn't ask you out, there's a reason.

SECTION THREE

LOOKS, ATTITUDE, AND

Confidence

CHAPTER 16

Most Freeing Concept Ever

Men Know in a Nanosecond Who Their Dream Girl Might Be

Wait for the man who likes your type.

Men are visual, and they have types. Faster than you can notice a man, he's already scanned the room, and he knows who he likes. When he's looking at photos on an online dating site, he knows instantly. A man's psyche is either into you or it's not.

Biologically, men are more visually stimulated than women. This is a crucial point to understand about men. Think about how visual you are — how much a man's outer appearance has an impact on you — and realize a guy cares more than you about the outer aspect. To get the type of courtship and romance I write about in this book, a man must be attracted to your type. When a man isn't asking you out or moving things forward, it could simply be that you're not his type.

You could be tall, thin, and blonde with a gorgeous face, yet if a man isn't interested in skinny blonde women — perhaps he's interested in curvier brunettes — he won't be as into you as he would be interested in the woman who is his type.

And while physical type is important, there's a lot you can do to keep up your appearance and dress hot for your boyfriend (or husband). Even if you're a man's type, you can't let yourself go. (Included next, in Chapter 17, are specific tips.)

If he's not attracted from the start, the spark will never ignite into a fire that lasts a lifetime. A man's physical attraction won't grow if it's not there in the beginning. It needs to be there right away or else the relationship will never be romantic, filled with chemistry and sexual tension. The sooner you accept this fact, the quicker you can find your Mr. Right who adores and appreciates you in a loving and romantic way.

Many women think they can turn a lackluster man around if they love him harder. Unfortunately, it doesn't work that way. You may scratch your head, wondering why a guy is crazy in love with a certain woman.

There are lots of traits that turn a man on. But it all starts with physical type. Then you need to do the best with what you have, never letting yourself go.

For women used to being in charge of their careers and every other aspect of their lives, this can be frustrating, because you have to wait for the guy who is attracted to your type to approach you. You can't make the first move and ask a man out. (Refer back to Chapter 5.) Many women try to win men over by working hard at it, like they work hard in school or business. They end up in tortured, unrequited relationships because of this.

Once you understand the importance of type, you'll become a dream girl to a great guy because you'll hold out for the one who likes your type. You won't pursue men because you'll realize it's a waste of time.

Men do marry women they're not attracted to sexually. Men and women marry for a variety of reasons, and sexual chemistry and physical attraction aren't necessarily present or part of every relationship or marriage. But if true romantic love is what you're holding out for, wait for a man who is interested in your type.

The best way to know if a man likes your look is to wait for him to approach you and ask you out and wait for him to jump through the hoops I discuss in this book. The guys who aren't feeling a strong attraction drop off quickly, or they won't approach you to begin with.

For women, a spark can develop over time. I've known many women and clients who have met guys they weren't attracted to initially, and then after a few dates, the women were gaga over them. They fell in love between their ears. That doesn't happen with men. Men know right away whether you're that woman that they have to have. A man falls for you initially with his eyes. For a man, the spark has to be present right away.

"Guys know in two seconds," said Billy, 38, a carpenter from Arizona. "Scratch that. It's even less than that."

You can't convince a man to fall for you by being brilliant or by telling him stories that make him laugh or make him realize what a loving person you are.

Not All Men Want Sex With You

Realize, too, that just because a man is a man, it doesn't mean he's interested in sleeping with you. Some men don't want the bother, even if you serve yourself up to them on a silver platter. I've interviewed many men on this topic, and many say there are times—when women have made it easy for sex to occur—when they aren't going to go there. "It's not worth dealing with the aftermath," one man said to me. "She invited me over for dinner and wine and made overtures, but I didn't want to deal with her afterward."

In many ways, women have a lot of power over men. But it only works when the man is mesmerized by you, and for that to happen he has to *feel* that spark. Some women think if they stare into a guy's eyes and give him an "I want to have sex with you" look, that he can't help but be turned on. "After all, he's a guy. He won't turn down sex," I've heard women say.

Yes, the male sex drive is strong. But a man doesn't want to sleep with any and every woman indiscriminately, and when he does sleep with women indiscriminately, it's because he wants sex and isn't interested in the real you. If a man isn't into you from the start, no amount of hinting about sex or your naked body is going to turn him into a prince. It may lead to a hook-up, but not the relationship of your dreams.

Being sexually suggestive comes off as aggressive and desperate. He may take your comment as an invitation to sleep with you, but the chase is *over*. If he's interested in you romantically, there's no need to hint about being naked. He's already picturing it.

Celebs And Models Get Rejected, Too

If you're a model, great. But if you aren't, it doesn't matter. Not all men want supermodels. Some do. But others like the girl next door. Some want blondes, others, brunettes or redheads. Some are leg men and others like breasts or your backside. Some will want you. Others will want your best friend. While others will want your co-worker or boss. Some men aren't going to like you, no matter what. You could look like Iman, Irina Shayk, or Gigi Hadid and there will be a man who will reject you and want a different type.

Models and actresses and other high-profile beauties have heartache, heartbreak, and headaches like everyone else. Princess Diana of England got Prince Charles, but he was in love with Camilla Parker Bowles, who was 14 years older than Diana. The tabloids and others considered Camilla frumpier than Diana. Yet I believe Prince Charles has that spark with Camilla that he didn't have with Diana.

Some gorgeous celebrities have disastrous relationships with men because they have no self-esteem and let men walk all over them. While they can attract a guy, they lose his attraction quickly because they're needy, controlling, or desperate. Men love mystery, and even the beautiful and famous need a good dating strategy.

Sometimes beautiful high-profile women have the opposite problem — they have inflated egos. They may think that because they're gorgeous and rich, they can get any man on the planet, even one who isn't interested in their type. They think they can win him over with their star power, but that doesn't work, either.

Imperfections Aren't A Dealbreaker

When you're with the right guy, he'll see you as his dream girl, and it won't matter if you have physical imperfections. Someone I know once complained to a male co-worker that she hated her wrinkly elbows, and he said, "No guy is looking at your elbows. They don't care what anyone's elbows are like. They're looking at three things," he said, meaning chest, legs, and backside. I'm sure he intended face to be part of the equation. But his point was that a guy would barely notice her supposedly imperfect elbows.

You should also work on inner acceptance and loving the body you have. That goes a long way. Try to never compare yourself with others, even models or Instagram babes. Realize supermodel Cindy Crawford doesn't look like Cindy Crawford all the time.

Don't get down on any perceived defects. Work with the

body you have now, even if you aren't happy with it. Most women are hard on themselves and worry about every minor or major flaw. The angst over that imperfection could be better spent on something more productive. You could get your bum in shape by doing 10 minutes of walking up and down the stairwell in your apartment building. Or you could find a YouTube video on how to create a smoky eye look.

Instead of letting your physical imperfections get you down, work with what you have while also working on being the best you can be on the outside. Even if you think you have many flaws, there's a lot you can do to be appealing to men. (Find more tips in Chapter 17.)

Waiting Is The Hardest Part

Not all men attracted to your type are going to pursue. Some men may love your type, but they are either spoiled, lazy, not ready for commitment, or it might be something else.

He may be a wolf in sheep's clothing. He may be emotionally shut down. He may be a loner who never wants a real relationship with anyone. Not all men want the type of intimacy and relationship you want. He could also have unresolved feelings for someone else.

Don't give up when you hit a rough patch or a dry spell. It's worth waiting for true lasting love with a man who loves and adores you. It isn't every day you meet a single man who you're attracted to who sees you as his dream girl and who pursues you.

Focus on what you can control. While you can't be aggressive when it comes to making the first move with a man, you can and should be aggressive about being the best you can be on the inside and outside. You should be aggressive about figuring out ways to get out there—i.e. online dating, asking for setups, and going to venues to meet men. Take massive action in getting out and about to meet Mr. Right.

Grow in your understanding of men so you can weed out time wasters, know how to communicate and act around men, and how to look feminine and appealing to men. You must also be serene and learn to let things roll off your back.

Men And Women In A Nutshell

At cocktail parties, people love to ask about my career as a dating expert. The single ones bring up online dating and pepper me with questions. I often explain how different men and women are online: "Initially, men mainly care about photos. And women have a long list of criteria."

A man's wish list is mainly related to a woman's looks. A man knows right away if he likes a woman based on her photos. He's hesitant to go on a date if he doesn't see a full body shot. Men tell me they don't like it when a woman looks angry in her online photos. They also tell me they get annoyed if they go on a date and find out a woman's online dating photos were from the 1990s.

Women certainly care about appearance, but to a lesser extent than men. Women also care about the type of career a man has. They get annoyed if he has terrible grammar. They think he's a cliché if he has photos with a big fish. They think he's a playboy if he posts snaps with other women. They think he's missing a sensitivity chip if he has pictures posted of his children. The list goes on and on.

Men and women approach dating and relationships differently.

The Bottom Line

Understanding that men have types saves women time because they hold out for the guy who likes their type. They don't waste time with men who are lukewarm about them. This also helps you become more confident because you realize it's nothing personal. It's just the way it is. You can just shrug your shoulders and say, "I'm a short blonde, she's a tall brunette, so he must like tall brunettes. I'm gorgeous but just not his type. There's nothing I can do about it except wait for the guy who likes short blondes."

All you need to do is be the best version of you and there will be someone you like who will be gaga over you, and that will be the beginning of a beautiful courtship. When you wait for the man who wants your type, you end up with a man who is so into you, so attracted, and feels so great around you that he will pursue you.

Dream *Girl* Dialogue

Here's how to respond if a man asks you out.

If a dark-haired tall man—totally your type—walks across a crowded room and starts talking to you and then asks you out, say, **"Um ... okay!"** Even if a man is not your type, I suggest giving him a chance. You could start falling for him. (If you're not attracted to him to the point that you can't even stand talking to him, obviously you can nicely turn him down.)

The fact that he walked across a room and picked you is a good sign, and this means he'll probably be motivated to keep things going. Don't talk too much or say, "I was wondering if you were going to come over to talk to me. I like tall guys, and you're one of the few tall guys here." The mystery will fade. All you need to do is agree to a date. If you act too overjoyed or help him ask you out, you'll interfere with the courtship that's supposed to happen.

CHAPTER 17

Femininity Drives Men Wild

Dress Like a Tomboy, and He'll Treat You That Way

Dress for men, not other women.

If you want to date the man of your dreams, dress feminine and look as good as you can. This might be obvious. But this needs to be said because too many women underestimate the power of femininity, and they don't dress to impress men. Even if you are a man's type, you may not be doing all you can to attract a man. For example, say a man likes short redheads with green eyes and freckles, and that's you exactly — but if you walk around in grungy sneakers and messy hair and no makeup, you might not attract the caliber of man that you want.

Even when you are a man's type, you should dress and groom in ways that will turn a man on. If you want to keep your guy drooling, dress the part. Dressing the part keeps the courtship and spark alive.

Some women dress for other women — friends or frenemies. They want to prove they have great fashion sense. Some women dressed for their moms growing up. They carried that over to adulthood and never learned how to dress sexy.

Be careful who you listen to in this department. You'll

get a lot of advice on your appearance. From your artsy hairdresser to your well-meaning, strait-laced mother, and younger, cooler fashionista daughter. Many people will have an opinion on what looks good on you. You may not want to listen to any of that advice.

Instead, do what works for men. That is, if you're single and want to be in a relationship with an attractive masculine guy. (Or if you're married and want to continue to keep that fire going.) Looking good will attract a man, and keeping a spark alive with a boyfriend or husband will make him happy, and you'll be happier and more confident, too. There will be a man who likes your type. (See the prior Chapter 16.) But you do need to work with what you have and be the best version of yourself. Some women think it's shallow to worry so much about their appearance, but it's not. It's the smart way to get what you're looking for.

You want your look to turn him on during that first meeting so all he can think about is how he's going to convince you to go on another date. It keeps that spark alive during your courtship. He'll think of you as a famous actress being chased by the paparazzi who chose to spend Saturday night with him.

Single men looking for single ladies are more turned on when you dress the part. Putting on makeup and wearing heels, tight jeans (but not too tight), and a short V-neck top (or tight top that shows some skin and hugs the body) signals to men and the universe that you're ready to meet a great guy. That physical attraction also keeps the spark alive in a long-term relationship or marriage that starts to get routine.

Checklist Of What Men Like

Remember, there are many things you can do to improve your look so that you'll be more alluring, feminine, and sexy to a man. I gathered these tips while working professionally with men in my capacity as a matchmaker, while coaching women all over the world as a dating coach, and through personal observations.

When I was a matchmaker, I'd show men photos of potential candidates. Before meeting a woman for the first time, photos were the most important thing to most of the men I worked with and to the hundreds of men I polled for this book.

While trends will change, these tips are timeless and always in style:

Long hair is key. Long hair biologically signifies youth. It's a turn-on to men. If you have difficulty growing your hair for whatever reason, get extensions or a wig. Long healthy hair helps you feel and act feminine. Some women in their 40s, 50s, 60s, and beyond tell me they think they're too old to have long hair. I don't agree, and the majority of men wouldn't either.

Choose classy sexy. There's a fine line between slutty and sexy, and that's classy sexy. Show skin—but not an excessive amount. Showing a little cleavage is okay, but don't show too much. Don't wear an extremely low-cut top with an exceptionally short miniskirt. That can look cheap. If you're going to wear a miniskirt, wear it with a tank top or a cute camisole top that doesn't go overboard on the cleavage.

Take pride. Looking put together is a reflection of how you feel about yourself. Men notice if you're wearing old clothes. They notice ripped, wrinkled or dirty clothing, with stains, pills, or threads hanging off. Also, don't wear vintage clothing on dates. Vintage is old energy and doesn't give off a hip vibe to a man. If you love vintage clothes, don't wear this type of attire around a man unless the item appears new and fresh. Save the vintage look for when you're with your girlfriends, family, or alone.

Add heels. Heels elevate your look every single time. Even when wearing jeans, your look becomes special in heels, your walk becomes sexier. If you have trouble with heels, you may need to practice walking in them. Or you may need to settle for a platform-type heel, which is typically more comfortable. Platforms are sexier than flats, so if this is the only way you can wear heels, do it.

Makeup is a must. It's important to wear makeup on dates and while getting photos taken for your online profile. Even better, wear it every time you leave the house, if possible. You could run into Mr. Right in an elevator. You don't want to appear garish, but you want to highlight your best features with cosmetics.

If you can pull off false eyelashes, do it. Or find a place

that applies permanent extensions. If you have money to splurge — before each Saturday night date — on a blowout at your hair salon and a makeover at your local makeup store, do so. Or, if you can only do it once in a while for special dates or events, that's great, too.

When you get a professional makeover, have someone take photos so you can have fresh ones for online dating. Or take a good selfie. (Make sure you're smiling.)

If you don't have money to spend on a professional makeup artist or at a cosmetics counter, take lessons or watch YouTube videos to create makeup magic on your own. If you're pale, bronzer or self-tanner makes a big difference. It gives you the sexiest, sultriest glow.

Add sizzle with fake fur, leather, and sequins. Men love fake fur — it's soft and sexy. A fake fur jacket or vest adds a dose of glamour and softness to your wardrobe. Also, a black leather pair of pants, a black leather skirt, and a black moto jacket are all musts. (Not at the same time, of course.)

Men also love sequins, studs, and metallic touches. Don't go overboard, but the right amount of sparkle is striking and sexy to a man.

Zippers add interest. Wear a zippered top, and a man's eyes go to the zipper. Zippers are also eye-catching on bags, boots, and jackets. Zippers add style to an otherwise basic staple.

Leopard is hot. Leopard is timeless. It worked when Golden Age of Hollywood bombshell Sophia Loren wore it, and it works when British model Kate Moss wears it today. This animal print adds a sexy, glamorous touch to any outfit, whether it's a belt, booties, or a coat. If you're a conservative dresser, you may not be ready to pull off a leopard coat, but it's something to work up to. Buy a pair of leopard booties and see how they feel. Then buy a top in leopard. As you get more comfortable, work up to a leopard coat.

Create sexy in a pinch. It doesn't take intricate and extensive steps to glam up a look. Once you have the basic outfits down, pulling together a sexy look quickly is effortless. Say you're invited by a friend at the last minute to a casual party and wonder, "What do I wear?!" All you need are tight jeans (darker wash works best on most people), heels, and a sexy top that shows some skin. Make sure you put on makeup, and you're good to go. If you've been getting regular blowouts and highlights and keeping your hair in good shape, plus working out, a glamorous look is easy to pull off without taking up too much time.

Don't forget jewelry. I love *The Rules* authors' advice, which is to wear a gold watch and hoop earrings. It's a very classy look. After a while, when you're seeing a man consistently, you may start to get bored wearing hoops all the time. You can change it up by wearing chandeliers and other long and dangling earrings.

Less is more. Just like with dating, heed the less-is-more mantra with clothing and accessories. Some women go overboard, ruining a look by adding too much jewelry or trying to do too much with one look. For example, you might have received a gorgeous heart-shaped statement necklace from your boyfriend. (By the way, this is an adorable and romantic gift and a good sign.) When you wear it, you may also decide to wear hoop earrings, bangles, a few gold rings, a gold watch, and a sparkly sequined gold belt. That's an accessory overload. A statement necklace is bold and can stand on its own, without any other jewelry, except the watch.

Be Careful With Florals, Prints, Color

Black is a great staple to wear to make a great first impression. For blind dates and a first online encounter, it's perfect because it's safe and sexy. As many New Yorkers already know — black is hip, elegant, and cool. It's always in style. It looks classy and chic on almost everyone. It also hides a multitude of sins and spills of coffee or red wine.

I tell clients to have a simple but sexy black outfit ready for their first dates. This way, they can focus on lining up dates and not worry so much about pulling an outfit together each time they have a first date. I recommend wearing black for the next few dates with the same man, too.

It's a good idea to have staples — a longer Lycra skirt, a shorter skirt, a leather skirt, leather pants, a V-neck tight top, a camisole top, a tank top, pumps, over-the-knee boots, high-heeled sandals, a wool peacoat, and a moto jacket — in black. When you have the basics, you're off to a good start.

While black is my favorite, other colors that work well are neutrals like beige, white, gray, navy, brown, or moss. When you get beyond a few dates with a man, you're going to have to mix things up. But this is a good problem to have. You can add bright colors, prints, and florals, doing so sparingly and carefully. Adding color can be tricky. You need to know what you're doing. Wear colors that flatter you, and make sure you don't go overboard with color. When you're wearing a floral dress, make sure it's something your grandmother wouldn't be caught dead wearing.

Experiment with florals, prints, and bright colors, but if you aren't sure, play it safe and stick with solids in black and other neutrals. The problem with florals and many prints is that they aren't always flattering on women. Plus, so many men have told me over the years that florals and other prints remind them either of drapes, couches, or outfits worn by their grandmothers.

Know your strengths and weaknesses. You can hide many of your problem spots if you know how to dress right. Even if you're overweight or have a body part that isn't in the best shape, there's a way to dress around problem spots. For example, while you're working on getting rid of a flabby tummy through diet and exercise, wear certain tops — like peplum in black or another solid dark color — that hide it or wear Spanx.

I love Sara Blakely, creator of Spanx. I want to give a nod to her here, not only because she created a solution to a problem that can help women in this crucial area. She's also inspiring. Follow her on Instagram, and you'll see what I mean. Her posts about persistence are often about life and business, but you can find motivation to help you keep going on your journey to find Mr. Right.

There will be certain items that won't look good on you

because you don't have the right body shape or it won't work with your coloring. As gorgeous as something is in a catalog or on a mannequin, if it doesn't flatter you, don't buy it. Or if you have an item in your closet that doesn't work, donate it to someone who will get use out of it. Doing so is great karma. Plus, you will make room for a better outfit — one with sex appeal — to come into your closet.

Hip, But Not Too Hip

You should be hip and stylish, but make sure you're not wearing anything too costumey or clownish. While couture items are beautiful, they aren't the type of items that necessarily attract men.

What might be exciting and fashionable to a woman — like a colorful, high-end Gucci dress with fancy fabric galore — won't necessarily turn a guy on. You should keep up with styles and be hip because men want to feel like they're with the cool girl. But men aren't as into labels as women, and anything too fashion-forward, like an avant-garde outfit you would see on a Milan runway, isn't sexy to a man.

For example, in 2020, puff sleeves were in. They're cute and stylish. But beware of over-sized sleeves that look like they're from Mars.

Some women feel that if they follow these tips they won't be able to express themselves through clothing any longer. On the other hand, these same women are coming to me, asking me what they can do to impress a man and what to wear on dates, and this is the best advice for that. My suggestions add up to a sexy look that turns a man on. If you feel like expressing yourself through clothing, do so when you're with your girlfriends, family members, or alone. When you're with your guy, follow these tips.

Also, sexy doesn't have to be expensive. Instead of spending $3,000 for a Balmain dress, that money would likely be better spent on a less-expensive clothing item from a hip website or shop.

Other things women spend crazy money on are bags and shoes. Beautiful bags and gorgeous footwear are status symbols among women. If you have the money for a $49,000 Birkin or a $2,000 Louis Vuitton bag or Christian Louboutin sandals costing $7,000, go for it. But if you can't afford it, it won't matter to most men. Use that hard-earned money on what matters, like a personal trainer, appointments for blowouts, waxing, self-tanning, cosmetics, manicures, pedicures, and beauty procedures.

I've never overheard a man say, "Wow, love her Birkin bag, is she single?"

The Best Way To Get A Second Date

I was once interviewed by a women's publication *Elite Daily* on the topic of, "How to Get a Second Date So You Won't Be Forever Alone."

The reporter wondered if perhaps touching a man in specific ways would turn him on so much that he would ask for a second date. Thinking this way is a mistake. Touching a man or staring at him suggestively might give him the invitation to move things forward sexually. Or, it could end it right there. He might sense desperation.

One of the best things you can do is look hot on your date. Being easygoing, nice, and confident are very important. Understanding men and following courtship strategies are extremely important as well. But it all starts with your appearance. Of course you have to be his type, but if he asked you out, you're probably his type, so you're on the right track.

Looking hot on a first date with a guy seems obvious. But many women aren't doing all they can in this area. Many women dress down on a date. They're beautiful but dress casually, with flats, messy hair, and no makeup. They think that a guy should love them for them. They think, "If he doesn't like me for me, then I don't want him."

But aren't you attracted to a man, on some level, based on his looks? It's only natural he'll judge you in the same way. And, as I explained before, because men are more aroused by visual stimuli than women, physical attraction is even more important to men.

The big secret that most contemporary women don't get is that you don't have to do much at all to let a guy know you are interested in a second date. There are so many theories from dating experts as to how to act on a first date to get a second date that it boggles my mind and has me worried for people who follow the advice that encourages you to actively lobby for a second date. The way to let a guy know you would like a second date is to answer, "Sure," when he asks you out for a second date. If he likes you and he wants to see you again, he will try to ask you out.

Can You Look Too Good?

Sometimes a woman will tell me she doesn't want to dress too sexy for a guy on a blind date or first meeting because she doesn't want to give him the wrong idea. I agree, especially when it comes to a first meeting — when you're meeting a stranger, through an online date or a setup. You should dress up, look amazing, but err on the side of being more conservative than you might after getting to know this man. Once you start liking a guy and getting a good feeling from him, you can turn on the sex appeal even more.

For example, on a blind drink date in winter, one woman I know wore tight dark-washed jeans, booties with a high platform heel, a tight black Lycra long-sleeved top with a jewel neck-line that had a slight cut out near the cleavage area, and a peacoat with a scarf. "It was freezing out, and I figured, I might not even take my coat off if the guy was a creep," she said. "It turned out I enjoyed talking to him and felt comfortable with him, so after a few minutes, I took my peacoat off."

Throughout their dates, she increasingly dressed sexier and sexier. On their 10th or 11th date, she wore a tight outfit with a plunging neckline and skinny high heels. She was falling hard and wanted him to fall for her equally as hard. At this point, too, she was more comfortable around him, and they were exclusive and close to sleeping together, so the sexy outfit was appropriate.

Many women worry about the extra attention they'll get if they look too good when dressing up on social occasions and at work. Some worry that other women will be mean to them if they look better than them. Others don't want the added distraction of being hit on all the time, so they prefer to dress very conservatively and plainly. Or they fear if they look too good, they won't be taken seriously in their careers.

Women should dress appropriately at work, then do a quick change before going on a date. I work with lots of smart and successful women who have busy careers. Some of them have to dress extremely conservatively at work. Many of them are going on blind dates or online dates after work, so I help them figure out ways to spark up the outfit. Depending on where you work, it could simply be that you need to put on more makeup and add a pair of high heels to jazz up your look. You may need to do more — in which case I would suggest bringing a change of clothes for the after-work date.

As for worrying about what other women think, I say, "What other people think of you is not your business." You have a worthy goal, and if you aren't hurting anyone, other women should mind their own business, too. The more you grow as a person and strengthen your insides, the more you'll realize it doesn't matter what people think. Your tribe of people will love you for you, as long as you aren't harming anyone. If you're beautiful on the inside and outside, there's no reason you should dim your sparkle or sex appeal to make other women feel secure. Staying small to help an insecure person feel better isn't fair to you or the lucky man who dates and marries you.

The Bottom Line

Dress for a man if you want to attract a man and keep him physically attracted. Men are visual and they like feminine touches. Dressing for men keeps the spark alive and makes courtship more fun. Sometimes all it takes is a few tweaks to add sex appeal to your look and to keep a man drooling.

Be careful not to dress for other women. Realize men aren't turned on by the same things other women are interested in. High fashion and high-priced bags and shoes aren't necessary to attract a man, either.

Dream *Girl* Dialogue

When you follow the advice in this chapter, men will compliment you and friends may critique you. Here's how to respond to both.

All you need to do when complimented on your look is smile and say, **"Thanks!"**

Get comfortable receiving compliments from a man, just like you receive his love. Practice receiving here, too. Don't push away a compliment from a man, saying, "Oh, this skirt, it's 20 years old, it's falling apart." He'll wonder,

"Maybe she isn't that special. Maybe she doesn't have cool clothes. Maybe she isn't the cool girl." Also, when you have a hard time accepting praise, you make the compliment giver feel bad.

Some people — friends or family or even acquaintances — may critique your clothing choices. Others may tell you to cut your hair. It's best not to get into a debate. There's no use convincing people who don't get it. It may take a lot of explaining, and even then, you may not win them over. If, for example, a friend tells you that you need to cut your hair into a bob because you're over 45, you can say, **"Thanks."** Hopefully, she'll let it go. Don't waste your energy getting into a debate or argument. And don't let her convince you to cut your hair.

CHAPTER 18

Men Respect Boundaries, Not Bitches

Boundaries are Healthy, But Meanness is a Turnoff

Make sure you have strong boundaries with men. But don't be a bitch.

If you don't have good boundaries when dating, you can get used by men and waste time. You should never be a doormat. But that doesn't mean you should be nasty or controlling because you'll turn off emotionally healthy men that way. It's important to stand up for yourself, but calmly and politely. This can be a difficult and delicate balance to get right, especially if you've never had good boundaries before. But if you start implementing these tips, you'll be well on your way.

Some women think they need to resort to being mean or rude to get a man to respect them and treat them like a princess. A woman may think nothing of saying to a guy after a fun date, as he kisses her on her stoop and asks to come inside, "Who do you think you are? You think you're getting lucky tonight? Ha, think again. You have to work for me."

I understand why a woman might think she has to say

that. She wants to be respected and treated well, and rightly so. But that strong wording could put off a good guy. If you say something like this, he may never call again, and it's not because you wouldn't sleep with him. It could be because you scared him with your feisty attitude.

Other times, women put up walls, thinking they're protecting themselves, but they go too far. Women who have given too much in the past end up compensating by shutting down and not letting anyone in who could hurt them. Some women have relationships with unavailable men—it's their way of keeping distance from men and intimate relationships. You don't want to get to the point where you shut down; you want to stay open for an available and loving man. Yet you do need boundaries, even with a good man.

Many women tell me they think men like bitchy women. But what a healthy mature man is drawn to is someone with boundaries. Boundaries show a man that you are a high-value woman.

A man may fall for a beautiful woman who is mean, and she might keep him intrigued for a while. But if the woman is nasty, a healthy man usually realizes he made a mistake. And even if she keeps the guy, what fun is a mutually miserable relationship?

There may be times when you will have to bring up an upsetting issue or concern, such as a safety issue. The thing is, you need to be careful about how you deliver the words and what words you use. If your critique is mean, emotional, or negative, it won't be received well.

One client, Mena, 37, from Montreal, had to mention a safety issue to a man she was dating named Karl, also 37. When she began dating Karl, he was chivalrous, picking her up on Saturday nights and taking her to dinner. Everything seemed to go well, until one night after he dropped her off, he sped away as she stood by her door in her heels and a hot outfit. It was cold, and she was fumbling with her keys as he drove off.

She liked him but wasn't sure she wanted to go out with him again. Even friends and colleagues who dropped her off knew to wait until she got inside. Then she decided to cut him slack, thinking, "Maybe he's spoiled by other women and has no idea how to be around women." She wasn't ready to break up with him because she liked him a lot and he seemed to treat her right in many other ways.

I told her to mention it next time, as safety issues are important. Because this issue was troubling, she stayed online and attended events to meet other guys. The next time Karl dropped her off, she said something to him in a nice and calm way. This is how you stand up for yourself without being a bitch. You mention an unacceptable behavior, but you aren't mean about it.

After Mena mentioned this safety issue, Karl was on his best behavior in this area going forward. But they eventually broke up. The lack of care Karl showed by speeding off after dropping her off was symbolic of how he ended up treating her in all areas. Mena was glad she multi-dated.

Sometimes you can gently train a man. It may work. But if it doesn't, you can't coerce a man to do something. Either accept him the way he is or move on to someone else. (As we said in Chapter 12.)

There are endless scenarios that can cause a woman to want to lash out at a man, but it's better not to. One common situation happens when a man requests a last-minute date. A man will sometimes text late in the week to ask for a Saturday night date. He may call or text on Friday night, Saturday morning, or even late Saturday. The woman is annoyed and blows up at him because she hadn't heard from him all week.

Some men who like you will—in the initial stages of dating—wait until last minute to ask you out. They may be spoiled and may have never met anyone like you before. Just politely decline the last-minute date. Don't get angry. Some men aren't used to courtship, and they don't know they're supposed to plan in advance. Don't say, "Sorry dude, you lost out. I already made plans because you waited too long to ask me out."

Eventually, the guy who likes you will figure out he has to ask you out early in the week. Preferably, he asks you out at the end of your last date, or better yet, he tells you he wants to lock you in every Saturday night going forward.

When you turn down last-minute date requests nicely, eventually the good guys get the hint that they need to ask earlier in the week. Good men figure out fast what they need to do to be with you.

Straight Talk From Guys

When you're mean on a date—whether it's to a server who got your order wrong or a snarky comment about your date's hot secretary or a rant about a text that just came in from your boss—your date will wonder if he's going to be in the line of fire next. If you're going to flip out over something like a valet who takes too long to get the car, he's thinking, "Am I next?"

One topic many men brought up to me while I was writing this book is how women behave toward those who work in the service industry. Being nasty to a server who's waiting on you at a restaurant is something many men have repeatedly told me turns them off. He'll think you're petty, selfish, and unhappy. You don't want to be that spiteful, mean person who can't get along with anyone.

Even if the server does something wrong—or many things wrong—it's mean to attack that person or complain to your date about them. It shows that you're unhappy in your life if you can't overlook something as small as a wrong order at a restaurant. Being nasty to someone who is waiting on you is the antithesis of an easygoing mellow woman who a man can relax and feel good with.

Maurice, 46, from Italy, said, "Nobody wants to connect with somebody mean. Being nice to waiters, to strangers, about people in your past—that hints at someone who has evolved, at serenity, is prepared to move on and to give."

Lucas, 33, said that when a woman is angry on a date, it's a drag. "A guy doesn't want to be reminded of his mother when she was in a bad mood. Guys don't like bitchy complainers."

Bob, 58, agreed that being rude to people in the service industry and others is a huge turnoff. "As my mother once said, 'How she treats others is how she'll treat you.' A woman who doesn't treat people with respect is lacking in character. I feel it's important to be courteous and respectful."

Jon, 60, said an attractive woman he has chemistry with can end up being a turnoff if she's angry, controlling, mean, or miserable. "When they complain to the waiter, or show anger at people when we're out, it's such a turnoff," Jon said. "Being a snob is a turnoff, too. Even if she's beautiful, a bad personality is tiring. Even if I'm attracted to her, I'll have reservations about moving a relationship forward."

Don't Stay Friends With An Ex

Because this chapter is about boundaries, I want to mention a key issue. Be careful not to stay close to an ex or anyone who may have hurt you in the past. Often, people with loose or dysfunctional boundaries stay too close to their exes, and this can be harmful.

If you have children or have to work with an ex-boyfriend or ex-husband, it's nice to have a cordial relationship. But beyond that, find friends and support elsewhere if a healthy and happy relationship is what you desire.

If you aren't with Mr. Right, you should be looking for Mr. Right, not wasting energy with an ex who may have hurt you badly. Even if your ex didn't hurt you, it's best to move forward. An ex-boyfriend or ex-husband is usually an ex for a good reason. You only have so much energy in a day, in your life, and you should be using it to create new and healthy relationships. Don't take the lazy way out, leaning on and spending time with a person who it never worked with.

Staying too close with an ex can mess with a current relationship or prevent you from getting into a healthy new relationship. It's not worth ruining a good thing to keep something that wasn't working in your life.

I see too many women clinging to exes—who were very bad for them—for financial perks, a shoulder to cry on, and help when they get into an emergency, like a car accident. That's what family and friends and AAA are for. If you're having problems with your current boyfriend, the last person on earth you should be talking to is your ex-boyfriend or ex-husband. If you're doing this, it means you need new and better friends.

This isn't to say you should be nasty to your ex. If you have to be in touch, you have to be in touch, but keep it at a surface level.

And there's no reason for a woman to give an ex a gift for a holiday or any other occasion. Unless you're divorced and you have a five-year-old son together and your child wants to give Daddy a gift for Father's Day or another special occasion. Beyond that, gift-giving to an ex is extremely unhealthy and evidence of poor boundaries.

If your ex is happy and in love, leave him be. It's bad karma to mess with a man who's taken. If he's a healthy guy who has moved on and is in a healthy relationship, he'll be happy you're leaving him alone.

And if he has a weak ego that needs to be fed by weird drama, why be part of that type of scenario? If he loves messed-up relationships, you may be feeding his weak ego by staying in his life, and he may be using your calls and presence in a sick attempt to make his current girlfriend jealous. You don't want any part of either scenario. You have your own beautiful life to focus on.

Also, when you strengthen your boundaries overall, you'll notice all relationships in your life will improve.

What if you run into your ex somewhere? If you don't have anything in common with the guy—no children in common or no professional reasons to be in touch—should you be polite? If he was a decent guy who treated you well, you can be cordial. But if the guy turned out to be a creep, steer clear. He doesn't deserve a second of your precious time. Don't squander the sexy!

My client Chelsea, 40, from Atlanta, came to me after struggling for years in the dating trenches. She was divorced, without children, and had a friendly relationship with her ex. They spent weekends together platonically on occasion. When she was in trouble—with a flat tire or needed help with flooding at her house—he was the first person she'd call. She didn't see things ever working out romantically again, but she relied on him a great deal, and since he was a nice guy, he was happy to help her out when he wasn't busy.

"I was lonely a lot after we broke up and it helped to still have that companionship," Chelsea said. "Instead of going to events where I could meet men, I would call my ex and ask him to have dinner with me. He was my crutch," Chelsea said. Sticking too close to her ex was using up valuable energy that she could put toward finding her Mr. Right. At first, she struggled to let go. But she decided to take my advice and move on because she wanted a serious boyfriend. She started building supportive friendships elsewhere and braving events alone. Meeting a new man is possible when you go out alone. But when you're with your ex, most men won't approach because it looks like you're on a date.

Within six months, she met a great guy after attending a happy hour alone. They've been dating for four months and she's glad she forced herself to move on. While she's cordial with her ex when she runs into him, she doesn't call him any longer when she's lonely or needs help. She has found other outlets, including me and a women's support group, where she vents when she is concerned about an issue involving her current boyfriend.

The Bottom Line

Having good boundaries is important to a healthy relationship. It's also critical to understand the healthy balance between standing up for yourself but doing so in a way that's not mean. Men respect women with boundaries, but meanness turns them off. When women understand this, they're more likely to end up in healthy relationships with men who respect them and treat them right.

Men also notice how you treat others. When a man sees that you're being mean to someone, whether it's someone in the service industry, a friend, or family member, he'll wonder if he's next in the line of fire.

Dream *Girl* Dialogue

It's vital to learn how to respond nicely in situations when you would prefer to angrily tell a man off.

If a man tries to sweet talk his way into your home after a date, don't tell him off. Instead, all you need to do while on your stoop after a guy kisses you and asks to come inside, is smile and say, **"I have an early day tomorrow. I have to go. Goodnight."** Then walk inside. Your actions make it obvious you aren't going to be a hookup. Decent men get the hint. If he explodes in anger, never see him again.

Here's a script to use if you're in a similar situation as Mena, my client whose boyfriend dropped her off at her house and then sped off. The next time he drops you off, say, **"Can you please wait until I get inside? I'm a safety freak."** You can use this verbiage for other similar situations that are concerning.

If a guy asks you out last minute, all you need to say is, **"I**

would like to, but I already made plans." Be gracious. He's asking you out. He's trying. He may not know much about courtship. Other women may have spoiled him. Don't be mean, but don't accept a last-minute date.

Don't tell a man what he needs to do to date you. "You need to ask me earlier in the week or else I get booked up," is something to avoid. If he wants to date you, he'll figure out what he needs to do to see you. When a man is motivated to see you, he cracks the case quickly.

If a server at a restaurant takes forever to bring your meal and messes up your order, giving you eggplant parmesan instead of chicken parmesan, never be mean. Nicely mention it with a smile, saying, **"Hi there, I ordered the chicken parmesan."** If you've ever worked in the restaurant business, you know how easy it is for mistakes to happen.

No matter the situation, think before you talk or text. Delaying is often a good tactic. This way, when you say something, you're more serene, and the words you choose reflect that composure. Deliver your message calmly and concisely. A man is more likely to listen when your words are shorter and less emotional.

CHAPTER 19

Looks Aren't Enough

Men Want the Cool, Confident Girl

Be confident. If you aren't there yet, fake it until you are.

Physical attraction gets the guy initially, and courtship keeps the spark alive, but you also need to be confident. When you understand men, you start to see that they're more likely to continue to court and marry a woman who's confident. If you don't think you're special, he'll wonder, too.

Even someone unhappy with their look, their credentials, or any aspect of their life can be confident. You can be a shy, overweight woman and be more confident than a thin, outgoing model. It starts with a choice that this is how you're going to operate in the world. Just like you should see the glass half full when it comes to your attitude about life in general, you do the same when it comes to your self-esteem. You see the good in yourself and focus on that.

Understanding men will also boost your confidence game. If you're reading and absorbing the concepts in this book, you're on the right track. Women who understand how men are wired are confident around them because there's no intimidating mystery to solve. You aren't pushing yourself on uninterested men. You only spend time with a man who wants you — and that fuels your confidence. You're more in control of your dating life and of relationships with men.

When you understand that some men aren't going to be attracted to your type, no matter what, you don't waste a split second worrying about them. You realize when a man doesn't love you, it's not personal. It could be that he's damaged. Or that you aren't a good fit. You haven't met Mr. Right yet. Once you accept and understand this, you can't help but be confident.

By following courtship strategies, you weed out men who would end up treating you shabbily, and you realize you could never go back. By holding back and allowing a man to pursue you and not accepting crumbs, you become more self-assured with men. When you adopt these courtship strategies, men who are supposed to be in your life step up and treat you well, and that, in turn, gives you more confidence.

Also, when you follow the strategies that I outline in this book, you become your higher self, and that leads you to be more confident because you become quite the catch.

You work on your outsides, too, which fuels your insides. The two complement one another.

Confidence starts with a belief that you're worthy because you're you and you're doing the best you can with what you have. Even if a guy you like ends up rejecting you, you realize there's someone better to take his place. You tell yourself, "It wasn't me — it just wasn't meant to be."

It starts with a choice that you're as deserving as anyone else. That you're just as good as anyone else, no matter what station of life you're in. If you are suffering from lack of confidence, I recommend you go to the spiritual gym, a place where you can build up your insides. Not only will doing so improve your confidence level, but it will make you happier in general. At the end of this chapter, I include a section that explains more in detail how you can nourish your insides by going to the spiritual gym.

How To Fake It Till You Make It

Some women are born with confidence while others can cultivate it. If you grew up feeling unconfident and were treated badly by men or people in general, your confidence level and self-esteem may be low. But there's no reason why it can't be built up. If you aren't naturally confident, you can choose to be. To start, act confident, even when you don't feel like it. Forcing yourself to take the right actions leads to confidence.

Many of you likely excel at many things. You have a fantastic career and successful life trappings. But you may be perfectionists and think that because you aren't perfect in every way, you aren't worthy of having a great guy.

That's a mistake. A guy is attracted to your look and that spark he feels when he's around you. He's not as obsessed with your perceived physical imperfections as you might be.

Also, a man isn't subtracting points because you make $100,000 less than another woman or because you got your master's degree at a state school instead of an Ivy League school. (The men attracted to your bank account or your college of choice aren't in it for love. Those drawn to you for materialistic reasons may be looking for a marriage of convenience or may be latching on to you for your money or your connections. To prevent yourself from attracting men who want you for these reasons, don't bring up your connections or your wealth.)

Even if you say something inarticulate on a date and feel silly, don't show you're embarrassed. If he likes you, he won't care. He may think it's cute. One client Megan, 38, a Beverly Hills native with an Ivy League education, was nervous while on a blind date with a cute guy with a Harvard Law Degree. She recalls saying something on their first date that made no sense. She didn't let her date know how stupid she felt, although she did confide in me after the date. "OMG, that guy will never call again, and I don't blame him!" she texted. Not only did he call her, but he chased her, and they had a beautiful courtship.

Even if you're insecure, learn to fake it till you make it, like Megan.

Drea, 30, from Connecticut, who is always trying to lose 30-40 pounds, acts confident when she's with her 25-year-old boyfriend, Christopher. If you saw her in action, you'd never know that she has insecurities. I ran into them one night at a party, and I felt like I was watching a Nicholas Sparks movie. He was gorgeous and claimed her right away by kissing her and holding her hand. She never critiques her body or mentions her insecurities about her age in front of him.

She doesn't compare herself to other women or make fun of them, either. A healthy mature man sees right through that. Right away, he thinks you're insecure or a snob.

Christopher picks up on Drea's confidence, and when he's with her, he treats her like a beauty queen. He makes her feel secure, and that fuels her confidence even more.

Copy Drea. Even when you aren't feeling hot, channel your inner hotness. It works.

"It's amazing how your 'Fake it till you make it' strategy works," Drea said. "I couldn't believe someone as cute as Christopher would fall so hard for me. I'm sure it a lot had to do with the fact that I acted like the cool girl around him."

Drea also works on her appearance. Even though she's not happy with her weight, she dresses hot, wears makeup, and spends time on her hair, keeping it long, soft, and shiny. She does the best with what she has. She also works out and is trying to lose weight. She followed my courtship strategies perfectly, pacing the relationship with Christopher from the beginning.

Most women tend to be more critical about their body than their man is, and the man doesn't get it. He thinks you're beautiful and doesn't understand why you're critiquing yourself. Never disparage your body in front of your man. Act like a model who he's lucky to see every week, and he'll treat you that way.

Men also lose patience when you go on and on about how much time you're spending working on your thighs.

The same goes for going on and on about your diet.

A 50-something businessman, Frank, from NYC, summed up the comments of many men I interviewed when he said, "When women go on about diet or exercise, I wonder right away if they're insecure." Frank added that diet and exercise talk can also be boring and sometimes feel "preachy." Some men wonder if you're looking down on them if *they* aren't on a diet or exercise plan. An exception is if he asks what sports you enjoy, and you mention how much you love spin class and tennis. But don't give him a detailed explanation of problem spots you're targeting through different weight machines and workout routines.

No One Likes A Show-Off

While you should be confident, don't go overboard in the confidence department. A man loves a confident woman, but not an arrogant one. Don't critique yourself in front of a man, but don't brag, either. If you have five other men chasing you, don't tell him. Let him wonder who is chasing you. If you tell him, it comes across as if you're trying to get a reaction from him, and that appears like a calculated move.

There's no need to show off in other ways, either. You don't need to boast about how well you're doing at work or how much you know about international affairs. While many men do want to be with intelligent women, they are turned off by bragging. Some smart and successful women who are confident in their careers think they're impressing a guy on a date by getting into intellectual debates about politics or world hunger. While he may be impressed by your intellect or debating abilities, he won't be turned on romantically. And if he did have an attraction, it will start to wane.

Guys want someone soft they can imagine coming home to and feeling good around. They get into enough debates at work or with family members. Some women think that by showing off their debating skills to a man, he's getting turned on by her intelligence, so they try to win the debate. But even if a woman wins the debate, she won't win him.

When online dating, the same concept applies. Beyond posting flattering photos, there's no need to brag. Too much boasting online comes across as insecure and desperate, as if you're trying way too hard to win men over. Some women write in their profile, "I'm the best girlfriend a guy can have, and your mother will love me," or "I bake and cook well, and my friends tell me I'm the most supportive woman they know."

When a man sees a woman trying too hard in any way, it turns him off. Trying too hard to impress a man intellectually or to make him laugh or fall in love with you is coming from a place of masculine energy.

Action Boosts Confidence

Sometimes you have to stumble a little until you get

to your goal. Don't let setbacks deter you on your path toward your goal or harm your confidence. Be thankful for your failures, for all the bad or nerve-racking dates and rotten men. You will look back and realize how all those experiences helped you become a better girlfriend and more confident.

Don't take rejection personally. If a man rejects you, he's not your guy. There's someone out there who is looking for you, too.

It may be hard to see it in the moment, but setbacks are learning tools that give you character. When you see them as learning opportunities and not failures, you won't let setbacks in the dating arena get you down. See any rejection as redirection — redirection to someone better.

Sign up for that singles event, even if you don't want to go. Take actions before you want to, moving through the fear. The more you take action, the more fearless you become.

Olga, 56, from Russia, came a long way in the confidence department. When we first started working together, her self-esteem was in the dumps, in part because her husband cheated on her with a much younger woman he met through work. Olga had a degree in fashion but gave up her career to raise her children, who had since moved out of the house.

She said, "I wanted to stay home and never leave, but I knew you were right, that I'd be happier getting out in the dating world and trying, even though I was afraid." Olga decided to look at her divorce as a learning experience that was redirecting her to something better. She had her down days, but she kept moving and taking social actions to meet men because she knew she deserved a better man.

She also decided she needed something in her life to be proud of, and launched a business designing attractive winter coats for women, something that had been a dream of hers before she got married. Having a new purpose in life made Olga feel more alive and raised her self-esteem, giving her more confidence in general, and that spilled over into her dating life.

Right before her first online date, which was at an upscale restaurant, Olga texted me while on the Metro, saying she was so nervous she wanted to throw up. She got through it, though, and when it was over, she texted again, saying, "It wasn't that bad." It's been six months, and Olga still hasn't met *the one*, but she says she has more confidence when walking into a restaurant for an online date and in all social situations.

Tips From The Spiritual Gym

As I've explained, just like you should be working out your body and taking care of it, you should also be working on keeping your insides healthy and strong. Doing so will fill you up inside, so you're a more confident and healthy dater.

Whatever spiritual tactics you use to help you get through the tough parts of dating will also help you while in a serious relationship with a man. All this inner work will make you a better girlfriend (and wife).

Going to the spiritual gym will give you inner strength that will lead to more confidence. It will help you be more easygoing, where you let things roll off your back so that you aren't out of control emotionally in relationships. You learn to be content while dating and in relationships. You become a better person and are more accepting and grateful for what you have. You can't control your circumstances, but you can control your attitude, so I recommend working on your attitude so you're content and happy with wherever your life takes you.

Different things work for different people. Try to devote time each day to what works for you.

Some people find religion works for them, while others swear by 12-step support groups. Some people meditate, others journal, and some people read books and other spiritual writings every morning when they wake up. Others find spending time in nature makes them calmer and happier. Or they use mantras like Natasha did when she was feeling low and needed a self-esteem boost. (Her story is in Chapter 12.) Coaches and therapists are also valuable. So are gratitude lists and vision boards. Or do some combination of the above. And don't be afraid to search out other ways that may work for you. Try everything until you find what resonates with you.

Surround yourself with loving and supportive people, too. When you have supportive people around you who respect and love you, it's easier to feel confident and filled up with love.

It's important to have other things to keep you busy — whether you're single and dating or in a serious relationship. As you know, even Prince Charming isn't going to make you happy 100 percent of the time. A man shouldn't be your only passion. Make sure you have a life filled with purpose so you aren't entirely focused on and obsessed with the man in your life.

Being mysterious and pacing a relationship is much easier when you aren't bored or lonely. When you're busy and passionate about the other things in your life, it's easier to follow these strategies. You're happier and more fulfilled in general when you're passionate about something besides a man. Men find independence and lack of clinginess sexy.

Here's more information in detail about some of the mindset tactics discussed above:

Having faith is powerful. Whether or not you have a religious faith is your personal choice. If you do, it's a good place to turn when you're struggling. Not only do studies show that religious people are happier and less depressed, but religion can also help you forgive and find peace with life's vicissitudes, as well as provide a like-minded support network.

Twelve-Step groups help many. Just like having a religious faith gives people a sense of connection, so do 12-step groups. That is just one of the benefits to a recovery program. The first 12-step fellowship was Alcoholics

Anonymous, founded in 1935, and since then there have been many offshoots, including groups for children of alcoholics, those suffering from food addiction, debt addiction, and many more. The 12-step support groups include a spiritual component, and promise a spiritual awakening as a result of the steps.

Journaling is rewarding. It's an easy way to get your feelings out. Say, for example, you're stressed about a certain guy you like and are wondering whether he's going to call again — you may find that writing your thoughts down will relieve some of the emotional pressure. Something like this is a good start: "If not him, someone better. If he doesn't call and skips a Saturday, someone better will show up. I only want a man who wants to be with me on Saturday night."

Meditation can be miraculous. Not only can a meditation practice help you become more calm and centered, it is also a powerful antidote to stress. Stress can lead to a multitude of physical and emotional problems, and studies have shown that meditation can improve one's mood, alleviate physical pain, and much more.

Coaches and therapists are invaluable. You may need professional help from a trained therapist to get through serious mental health issues or other problems that are blocking you from living a healthy life. Coaching can be extremely powerful as well, and is where I learned many life-changing lessons that allow me to live an amazing life. Dating coaching, in particular, can help in many ways. (For example, my coaching services help women understand men even more thoroughly, guide them to implement the strategies in this book, help women avoid self-sabotage, and much more.)

Mantras keep you going. If the voice in your head keeps saying, "I'll never meet Mr. Right," replace it with another mantra — an opposite one like, "Mr. Right is right around the corner. He's looking for me, just as I'm looking for him."

Gratitude is gold. Gratitude lists fill you up inside, emphasizing the good things in your life and the good things in your personality and character, so you aren't as focused on the bad. If you're feeling low, a gratitude list can give you a boost and help you realize how many positive attributes you do have. Your list could start off like this: "I have beautiful, long hair that is youthful and attractive to a man. I am easygoing and know I will make a man happy. Because I understand men, I will be the best girlfriend/wife ever." The more grateful you are for what you already have, the more you will receive.

Create a vision board. Create an online one or buy items at a craft store and make one with poster board, glue, scissors, and magazine images. When you look at your vision board, pretend you are in it. Get so clear on your vision that you can see, smell, taste, and really feel it.

Books are a solace. There are a plethora of books out there that can help you through whatever is ailing you, whether you simply need a boost of motivation to keep going or whether it's a more serious issue. If you have anger issues or are having a hard time forgiving someone, or if you're suffering from jealousy or simply need to think more positively, there's a book for that. While one book might not solve your entire problem, books can be a starting point and a great comfort.

The Bottom Line

Confidence is a turn-on to a man. It will keep him chasing you during your courtship and beyond. If you don't think you're special, he won't either.

Realize you don't need to be perfect to be confident; men aren't looking for perfection. And while confidence is sexy to a man, arrogance is a turnoff.

Taking many actions while you "fake it till you make it" is a great strategy to implement on the path to becoming more confident. While taking actions toward your goal, you start to feel more and more confident.

Understanding men will help you to be more confident around them. When you learn how a good man in love behaves and how to weed out time wasters, you only end up with men who like you — and that gives you confidence.

Last but certainly not least, focusing on your insides by developing your mindset and nourishing your soul will also help while dating, and in all areas of your life.

Dream *Girl* Dialogue

Here's what to say and what not to say when accepting a

compliment graciously:

If a man tells you he loves your hair, all you need to do is smile and say, **"Thanks!"** There's no need to elaborate. Nor should you compliment him back. (Refer back to Chapter 14.) Some women may want to explain all the work they do to keep their hair looking amazing. Others might ask, "Do you really think so? I wasn't sure it looked so great today because of the humidity, and the extra product I put in flattened it out." At this point, he's tuning you out. The more you elaborate, the less he thinks you're special and the less confident you sound.

And here is how to boost your confidence with a mantra:

One way Olga pumped herself up when she felt insecure before walking into a singles-oriented venue was by telling herself she was a famous fashion designer who was always sought after by the paparazzi, especially now that she had just broken up with a Hollywood heartthrob. **"I'm a famous fashion designer and I'm on *People's* 100 Most Beautiful People list this year. I hope the paparazzi doesn't crowd me too much this time, I may have to have a 24-hour bodyguard."** The mantra made her smile, pumped her up, and put her in a good mood as she walked into the room.

SECTION FOUR

GETTING TO THE
Next Level

CHAPTER 20

Don't Treat Him Like a King

Save That for When He Puts a Ring on It

Don't be a man's errand girl, housekeeper, personal assistant, or cook.

Many women think if they treat a man like a king, he'll treat them like a queen. Courtship doesn't work this way. When you do too much for a man during courtship, it works against you.

You'll have plenty of time to treat him like a king while married. This is an important distinction. When married, you're committed and on one another's team. You should treat him like a king to keep your marriage flowing properly. Sometimes single women think that the things a wife does for her husband — like cooking for him, doing errands, and helping make his life run smoother — also work on single men. But, single men are different animals than married men.

During courtship, all you need to do is receive and see what he's capable of giving you. Before he puts a ring on it, even when you're in an exclusive relationship, he must court you and treat you special. By giving him space and doing less for him in the beginning, you're doing him a huge favor. You're giving him a challenge, which is so essential for that spark.

If you do too much for a man during courtship, you'll harm your relationship because you'll turn the relationship casual quickly. You kill the chase, and a man will start taking you for granted. You may even start to feel used by him, and if you do, it could be your fault.

Also, when you give too much early on, a man may wonder what you're trying to get from him. He'll wonder if you're trying so hard because you desperately want to marry him. He may even start to see your behavior as controlling and manipulative.

Sometimes a man will ask you to do favors, like housekeeping duties or errands, early on. Be wary.

Sometimes men who ask you to do favors are simply bad news. But other times, it could be your fault. If you don't follow courtship strategies, a man may feel like he has a right to ask you to do favors for him early on. Are you spending days upon days at his house? (A big no-no.) If so, a man may feel entitled to ask you to do errands for him and clean his house. You're acting like you're living at his house, so he may think he has a right to ask you to pitch in. This is why the once-a-week dating guideline in the initial stages of dating is so critical. (As we covered in Chapter 6.) During courtship, you don't want to be the casual girl. So if this is you, make sure to pull back and stop giving so much.

Sometimes the damage has been done, and if you've gone overboard it's too hard to correct your behavior to achieve dream girl status. But other times, you may be able to salvage the relationship if you start pulling back and begin to adhere to these courtship principles.

Giving Got Her Nowhere

Tatiana, 30, from Austin, came to me after a three-year relationship ended. She met Leo, 32, at a party hosted by mutual friends at her law school. She had just graduated, and Leo was still in law school. Tatiana had a fabulous job, making well over six figures at a big firm. Leo had been working as a server at a restaurant while in law school and had a full plate, including twins. She knew Leo had a lot going on and tried to help him. Besides paying his rent so that he could work less and study more, she cooked, paid for a cleaning lady, and helped him study. She paid his children's school expenses and bought them gifts. She watched his children on the days he had custody. She stayed overnight on some nights and had a drawer at his apartment.

Leo told Tatiana he'd think about having her move in when he graduated from law school. She said it was exhausting to cook and take care of his children and help him study, on top of her high-pressure job and taking care of her own apartment. But she figured that he wouldn't keep her around during the week and involve her so much in his life if he didn't think she was special. Tatiana also loved being around him and wanted to be part of his life.

She continued to act like what she thought was a good girlfriend until one day they got into an argument. Leo said, "I'm not sure you should come to the lake house with me and the kids this summer." She threw a bottle of her perfume at the wall. It landed on her Saint Laurent satchel, shards of glass and perfume spilling all over it. During that argument, after she pressed him, Leo told Tatiana that he didn't see a future for them together.

Ultimately, Tatiana moved on, but the split was beyond painful. She threw that expensive bag out because she was unable to remove the smell of the perfume. It reminded her how out of control her emotions were. The bag also reminded her of how much time and energy she wasted on a dead-end relationship.

If you allow a man to take advantage, he may do so, as Leo did. Tatiana made his life better in that she paid his rent and helped him out in a way that a housekeeper, maid, or parent might. But she wasn't that special person he wanted to spend the rest of his life with. Leo took Tatiana for granted. Men need to work to get something or else they won't appreciate it.

As Tatiana was reeling from the breakup, she forced herself, even though she was suffering, to get back out there and start dating again right away. She was determined to get it right the next time around.

Today, Tatiana is married to an amazing guy, Marcus, who treats her right. But she had to make many changes, including keeping her emotions on an even keel and learning to weed out time wasters. When she met Marcus, who was smitten with her right away, their courtship fell in place perfectly because she paced the relationship. Before she got engaged, there were times when she wanted to cook for him and buy pots and pans for his kitchen, but she waited until they got engaged, with a wedding date set.

The Bottom Line

Doing too much for a man during courtship works against you. You'd think that doing more while dating — and showing a man what a good wife you'd make — would work in your favor and win a man over. But a man gets suspicious and is turned off when a woman tries too hard to impress him during the dating stages. If a man isn't working to impress a woman during courtship, it's not exciting for him, and he values it much less. A man will take advantage and take you for granted if you allow this to happen.

Dream *Girl* Dialogue

There may be a time when a man will ask you to vacuum his floors, take his car to get washed, or perform a similar errand. Simply giggle and pretend he's joking.

If a guy wants you to do errands or chores, he needs to put a ring on it. If he pushes you for an answer as to why you can't help, **"Sorry, I can't,"** will suffice.

He could be a bad news guy. Or perhaps you gave way too much too soon already, and he starts seeing you as "errand girl," not the "it girl."

There may be times when you follow these courtship strategies perfectly and a man will still ask you to do chores and errands. In most cases, and unless it's an exceptional circumstance, this isn't a great sign. This isn't a masculine man who is providing for you, protecting you, and wooing you. Seriously consider moving on from any man who sees you as an errand girl, housekeeper, or personal assistant. You want to be seen as a romantic lover who he needs to court and impress.

There may be a time when he's trying to integrate you into his life, and he may ask you to do something that seems on the surface like a chore, but it's a sign that he wants to move things forward. Still, be cautious about playing house with a man too quickly. For example, if he says, after two months of dating, "I want you to help me clean my closet so we can merge closets," reply, **"Oh wow, I'm not sure we're there yet."**

A man should respect that you're taking things slow. If this request came after a year, after an engagement ring, this is awesome. But two months in is way too soon to share his closet space. When you turn a man down for such a request, he'll see you as different and special because many women don't have the confidence or the knowledge to operate like this.

If it's eight months in and you're dying for a proposal— you know you want to be with this guy and want to be part of his closet—you can show more interest in combining your clothes with his, but you still shouldn't accept a request to come over and merge closets. Not until he puts a ring on it or gets close to doing so. Say something like, **"Oh wow, sounds cool, but I can't make it that day."** In this case, when it's eight months in, it's a good sign. But until you get a read for sure as to where things are going, as in serious talk about future intentions with an imminent ring, you shouldn't be merging closets. Depending on the situation, this could be a good time for a mini talk, asking what his intentions are. (See Chapter 22.) If the answer is a good one, and he proposes and sets a wedding date, YAY. It's time for you to think about merging closets.

CHAPTER 21

A Man Won't Tell You When It's Over

He'd Rather Scrub His Face with Comet (True Story)

Silence is all the closure you need.

When a man stops calling, let him go. You don't need to interrogate a guy as to why he's not stepping up to the plate. Nor is there ever a need to call him and ask, "Are we still on for this weekend?"

Men have a hard time telling women they aren't interested. Most men don't want to be the bad guy. They fear your anger and are afraid you'll become an emotional basket case. They don't want to have to face your tears or strong emotions.

Sure, there are men out there who will say something like, "Sorry, we're done." But many others feel bad telling you the truth.

As you know from reading this book, men, unlike women, don't enjoy having deep relationship-minded talks with women. This is especially true when they want to move on. When a man doesn't want to see you any longer, he wants the easy way out.

Relationships that start with promise can take a negative turn. You may start dating a man who asks you out on consistent Saturday night dinner dates. But after a few months, he starts pulling back. Early on, men also drop off without giving a reason. You may go on one fabulous date with a man and feel, based on that chemistry, that he's exactly what you're looking for. The guy says, "I'll call you," but never does. In both scenarios, let him go.

When a relationship starts petering out, you may think you need to give more. It's a normal human reaction to feel this way, especially when you have strong feelings for someone. This is when you need to listen to your head and ignore your heart.

Giving more won't get a man back on track in a healthy romantic courtship. Neither will confronting a man, asking him why it's over. Many times, women want an explanation. Some men give a breakup speech and others don't. Some men don't have it in them, unfortunately, so they disappear. Realize that silence is your answer, loud and clear. The best thing to do is move on as fast as you can. It's not worth wasting precious energy to win him back or get in an argument.

Some women feel like they need to initiate a conversation before they can move on. They'll text or call the man and ask, "What's up? Where have you been?" Or they'll say, "You can't break up without giving me a reason."

He may not respond. He may lie. He may tell the truth. The truth could hurt worse. He may say, "You aren't the one I want to spend the rest of my life with"; "I met someone else, and I want to move on and start dating her"; or "I'm just not attracted to you any longer and not sure I ever really was."

Whichever way you slice it, it hurts. But at least if you do nothing, you have your dignity. It's not necessary to have a big emotional blowout to find out what happened. The reasons don't matter that much in the scheme of things, even though you may be dying to know. What matters is whether he's in or out. Move on to someone who is all in.

Often, when a man wants to break up, he'll stop texting and calling. Or he'll start being mean and picking fights. A man finds it easier to pull back or cause problems, hoping a woman breaks up with him, rather than having to tell her, "It's over."

You can often tell when a guy is heading toward a breakup, even if he doesn't tell you. (Check back to Chapter 7.)

He may start asking you to pay. Or he'll stop asking you out for Saturday night dates. He may ask you to drive to him, and when you don't, he gets annoyed. His behavior may become abominable. He may look at other women in front of you, disrespectfully. Or insult you or start an argument.

Seriously consider whether you want to stay with a man who is trying to hurt you. This may seem obvious, but too many women make excuses for a man's bad behavior. They cut an abusive or angry man too much slack.

During a beautiful courtship, a man wants to impress you.

An interested guy continues to call, text, and pursue. He pushes forward. When you let Mr. Wrong go, he usually disappears. He may check in with you at times, but he isn't all in.

Even if a man is direct and says, "It's over," some women may cling to hope, trying to get him back. Many women think they can fix what's wrong. But when a man says he never wants to see you again, he's done.

When he's the wrong guy, there's nothing you can do or say to make a relationship happen. It's easier to let him go. You'll keep your self-respect intact. One client, Calista, 43, from New Mexico, found this out the hard way. She thought Keith, 53, a man she met through a friend, was *the one* because he treated her so well early on. He had all the traits she was looking for. She felt a deep connection. "OMG, I think he's going to be my husband. I have never said that before!" she said after their fourth romantic date. He showered her with gifts and kisses and called her "special," "hot," and "different." Keith paraded her around to everyone in his life. He introduced her to high school friends, family members, his children, work friends, and neighbors.

But after a few months, Keith started skipping weekends and then asked Calista out for Sunday night instead of Saturday night. When she declined a Sunday night offer, he disappeared.

Keith never contacted her again for a date. Calista was heartbroken. She said that she felt like there should have been more closure. She texted him, describing him as "thoughtless and rude." She was even more incensed that he ignored that text. So she fired off another text, telling him, "Who do you think you are? What kind of jerk dates a woman for so long and then drops her? You're a real low life, you realize that, right?" He responded, but got angry and said hurtful things, like, "It wasn't there, the chemistry wasn't there," and "If you think I'm such a jerk, you're better off without me. Why don't you just LEAVE. ME. ALONE!" Calista was so devastated by this text exchange, she wished she had let him go without reaching out.

You may run into a man in the dating trenches like Keith, someone who turns on the charm in the beginning but who doesn't have serious intentions. A guy may think you're beautiful and date you because he loves the chase. He may have just broken up with someone when he met you and needed a distraction, and you were fun for a while but not *the one*. You may not have been his type, and he dated you because he had nothing else going on. He might have had a fun first date but didn't feel enough for you to call for a second date.

Whatever it is, learn from each encounter, and move on with dignity fast.

How Far Men Go To Avoid Being Honest

My friend, Nathaniel, 55, told me a story from his dating past that is a great example of how hard it can be for a man to be truthful. While this scenario occurred after Nathaniel's first date with the woman, men at all stages of relationships have difficulty telling a woman when it's over. It's a dramatic example but one that illustrates how hard it can be for men to tell the truth.

Nathaniel says a colleague fixed him up on a date with a woman, and they went out for drinks. He knew within "one second" it wasn't going anywhere. It wasn't that she was unattractive, but she was unattractive to *him*.

"I didn't like her voice," he said. "We parted and said we'd see each other again — me having no intention of that," Nathaniel added. She called the next day, asking to meet him. He didn't want to see her again, so he made up an excuse, but she kept pushing. "I said I had a bad sunburn and couldn't get together. She insisted and headed over."

He panicked. He was afraid she would get angry when she saw he didn't have a sunburn. "I jumped in the shower and started washing with Comet," he said. "I wanted it to look like a sunburn." He scrubbed hard, until the Comet, an abrasive powder used to clean stubborn surfaces, turned his face, arms, neck, and shoulders red. The woman arrived at his place, and he told her again he wanted to be alone. He told her he wasn't interested in hanging out because he didn't feel well and had a sunburn. Nathaniel said she refused to give up, telling him, "You look fine." Then, she dropped her overnight bag on the floor.

Nathaniel said even though she slept over — at her insistence — he didn't have sex with her that night. "I wasn't attracted enough," he said. Nathaniel says he should have been more up-front. But he said telling her straight up that he wasn't interested was too difficult.

Don't be the woman who doesn't read the signs.

Closure Convos Don't Bring Closure

Even when a man tells you why he wants to end a relationship, he's not always honest. Sometimes a guy will say he can't commit because of an emotional or psychological issue. He may blame it on his "baggage."

Sometimes a woman sticks around, thinking if she helps this man, it will be a win-win. She thinks she'll get him over his problem, and he'll be so impressed at how supportive she is, he'll stay. But it doesn't work this way. When a man feels like he needs a trained therapist, he'll find one.

When you demand to know why he can't commit, he might give excuses. For example, he may say he's struggling with a childhood issue or damage caused by an ex-wife. He may tell you he's in therapy working on his issues and can't commit because of it. Or he may say that his custody situation is complex, and it would be too hard to fit you into his life right now.

He may tell you the unvarnished truth—that he's not feeling it with you, and never did. This could hurt worse than an excuse. When you don't let a dying relationship go, you may end up in an argument, like Calista did, where a man says hurtful things. Even if his answer is truthful, there's no use convincing him you're meant to be together. You deserve better. *He* should be convincing *you* that he's the right man for you.

I can't tell you how many times I've heard a guy give a woman an excuse like, "I'm not marriage-minded," for why he can't be with her. Then six months later, he's married to his Mrs. Right.

Everyone has "issues" and "baggage," although some more than others. When a man finds someone he loves, he wants to be with her. She makes any issues or baggage more manageable. She makes him feel alive and that all things are possible. The spark he feels for her might even cause him to put energy into tackling his problems on a deeper level.

Don't Get Strung Along

A man may try to have his cake and eat it, too. Sometimes a relationship starts off right but then starts to peter out, and instead of ending it, a man will try to keep you in his life but on the back burner. He won't tell you this, but if he's only seeing you once or twice a month, he's likely got a rotation going. Or he's going out, intending to meet someone else. He's not all in any longer, if he ever was.

If you try to force a guy to revive a relationship, he may keep you around for sex or friendship. But you'll never be his dream girl.

This can be confusing for women. You may think he's interested because he is sometimes available when you ask him out. Yet, he's not moving things forward. Or, he might try to call you last minute on Saturday afternoon and get you to go out with him on Saturday night. He won't plan in advance any longer because you're only a last-minute thought. Guys do this when they're bored or when plans fall through. He may be missing you a little. He could be missing the sex. When this happens, stay strong. Never accept a last-minute date. Don't allow a guy who checks in sporadically to mess with your head. And don't read anything into "Happy Thanksgiving," "Happy Holidays," or "Happy New Year" texts from men you haven't heard from in weeks. Men do this all the time due to boredom or when they need an ego stroking. You want to be with a man who wants to be in your life.

During the beginning of the 2020 COVID-19 pandemic, when people were confined to their homes, many of my clients were telling me they were receiving texts from men in their past. These were either men who broke up with them years ago or men they met online who never asked them out or men who they had a date or two with who dropped off. In every single case, my advice to these ladies was to ignore the text. You don't want a bored man in your life. You want a man who is gung ho about you, one who never lets you go.

It's Not Always His Fault

A good guy will start to pull back if you aren't doing your part in the relationship. What do I mean by this? If you're acting clingy, low vibe-y, and controlling, a man may pull back.

If the relationship started great and you blew it because you didn't understand men, you may have a chance at getting back your dream girl status by employing the strategies in this book and being the best girlfriend you can be.

Other times, it's over for good because too much damage has been done. Sometimes it's too hard to turn it around. You need to be your best self—both inside and outside—to get and keep a great man who properly courts you.

When you understand men and follow the courtship guidelines in this book, the right guy will treat you amazingly. But when you throw off the entire courtship process, don't expect a man to step up to the plate, and don't be surprised when he pulls back. Pay attention to the courtship strategies throughout this book and follow them carefully. Do your part, and then surrender to what is supposed to happen.

If a guy pulled away because you were being mean or demanding or difficult, you might be able to get the relationship back on track. But he may also decide he'd rather move on.

The Bottom Line

When you understand that silence from a man is an answer, you're no longer stuck day-dreaming about the potential relationship. You aren't obsessing over whether he likes you. The answer is crystal clear. You can move on to find Mr. Right. Other concrete signs include many of the concepts I've written about in the book, including whether a man sees you on Saturday nights, if he brings up a future, and how he treats you.

Never ask a man why he isn't asking you out or why he's pulling back. Try not to dwell on it. It's a waste of time. Yes, it may hurt. You may want to throw a fit and demand an answer from a man who ghosts. But it's better to move on with dignity and not give a man the satisfaction that he hurt you. Stay classy.

When you realize silence is an answer, you won't be scratching your head, trying to make it work with someone who's not that interested. You'll move on quickly to the man who wants you.

Dream *Girl* Dialogue

While there's no need to call a man to ask why he's pulling away or ghosting, there may be times when you'll be involved in a breakup conversation that he initiates. Here's a dialogue to use when he's ending a relationship or dating situation and for when he's trying to date you but treating you badly. I've also included scripts for when you may need to make amends, for when a situation isn't black and white, and for when you want to end it.

It's beneath your dignity to demand an answer as to why

a man is pulling back. So is fighting for someone who doesn't want you. Doing so is damaging to your self-esteem. It's a precious waste of time that could be better spent meeting Mr. Right.

If a man isn't calling to line you up for dates, there's nothing to say and no need to initiate a text to ask, "Hey, aren't we on for Saturday?"

If he does give you a breakup speech, say very little. When a guy's done, he's done. If you have to convince a guy to stay with you, he's not your guy. Say, **"Okay,"** or **"No problem,"** or **"I agree."** And move on.

Sometimes a guy who has one foot out the door will jerk you around. He's skipping Saturday nights, flirting with other women in front of you, talking about how he sees no future with you—yet he may still get angry that you aren't remaining part of his harem. He may blame you for this, saying, "You never call me enough," or "You should pay for dates sometimes."

When a guy keeps asking you out but treats you badly, ignore his texts or calls. Or to get him to go away, say, **"No thanks."** There's no need to get emotional or angry. Keep it classy and cool. If a man who is treating you badly wants to know more about why you won't continue to date him, just say, **"This isn't working out for me."** This guy is not your guy. No need to cry or lash out or give him a long speech. Again, getting into a big fight with a guy who wants out isn't worth the energy.

There may be a time when you need to make amends to a man because you were the one who behaved badly. Say, for example, everything started great and he pulled back after you started arguments and lashed out at him. Then you can say, **"I'm sorry I let my emotions get the best of me. My behavior was uncalled for."** See how he responds. He might be done. Or he might want to give it another shot. Don't get emotional when making amends. In general, a man will tune out a woman who is emotional and will even start thinking the woman is crazy.

Also, there are times during courtship that you'll encounter situations that aren't black and white. Say, for example, you're exclusively dating a guy who consistently asks you out and pays for dates and drives long distances to you every Saturday, yet he skips one or two Saturday nights to hang out with the guys. Don't contact him, saying, "Are we on for the following Saturday?" In this scenario, wait until he contacts you again for another date. He may never contact you again, so wait to see what happens. If he does call you to ask you out, tell him, **"I'm not sure this is working out for me."** When a guy who likes a woman hears that from her, he'll try to find out what's wrong. If a man wants to see you again, he'll say something like, "Why isn't it working out for you?" You can say calmly, **"I thought we were exclusive and seeing each other every Saturday. If not, I need to date others and move on."** No need to get emotional or angry or say much more than this. This message is clear. If he's feeling the same, he may say, "I don't want to date others. I want to be with you." Things may get back on track permanently. Or they could just get better for a while, and then get back off track. It's hard to know without playing it out.

The guy who isn't that crazy about you might not even respond when you say, **"I'm not sure this is working out for me."** Or, he may continue to skip Saturday nights. He may tell you he's not looking for something serious, which is good to know now because it frees you up. There's nothing more to say, as it's a waste of time and energy. You have a pedicure to get, an online dating profile to write, a weekend trip to Club Med to plan, and Mr. Right to meet.

Sometimes the opposite situation occurs. You may be the one who has to do the breaking up. Sometimes you don't have to say anything. You don't want to be a rude ghoster, yet there are certain situations where it's okay to ignore a man's text.

Say, for example, you went out once, and he texts for a second date. This early on, it's fine to ignore him. Usually, a guy gets the hint. If he's interested in you, he may persist more than once, trying to pin you down for that second date. In that case, it's a bit cruel to let him fly in the wind. This is a good phrase to let him know you aren't interested: **"I enjoyed meeting you, but I don't see us as a match,"** or **"I don't see us as a match. Good luck with your search."**

If you've been dating someone longer and want to stop dating him because you don't see it working out long term, it's only fair to tell him. It's basic human decency to explain as gently as possible why you're ending it. Dropping off the face of the earth isn't nice. Depending on how long you were together, you can say something like, **"The time we spent together has been great, but this isn't working for**

me any longer. I'd like to move on."

He may ask for specifics, and it's okay to give them if you feel he'll be able to handle it. For example, maybe you don't see how you can make it work because you come from different backgrounds. Then you could say, **"We come from different backgrounds. I don't see it working out."** He might try to convince you to stay. Make sure you're prepared for that. **"Sorry, I already made up my mind,"** is a good answer if a man persists.

Or maybe a guy has anger issues. He's never hurt you or been abusive to you before, but you want to break up because you don't feel at ease around him. In that case, say something like, **"I've enjoyed our time together, but I don't think our personalities fit. I want to move on."** If he persists in asking why, and you feel safe enough to say it around him, you can tell him that his mean streak is upsetting. Maybe you'll be the catalyst for him to get help with his anger issues, but don't let him convince you to stay. Men don't change that quickly. Whatever you say, say it shortly and sweetly.

CHAPTER 22

Rushing Ruins Relationships

But Don't Wait More Than a Year for a Ring

Don't rush a man.

This goes against courtship and turns women into pursuers. It's also controlling. But if you handle a man right and follow the strategies in this book, and if he's a good, marriage-minded guy who sees you as his dream girl, he'll move a relationship along in a timely manner. He'll usually have the exclusivity talk early on (in three months or before) because he wants to get you off the market. He'll treat you special on your birthday and Valentine's Day. He'll integrate you into his life and ask you to meet family members and friends. He'll talk of a future.

It takes strength to have confidence that a relationship will unfold the way it's supposed to, without you controlling things. But when you understand men, you realize that letting a relationship with a man play out on his timeline is the way to go.

Usually, when you leave Mr. Right alone and don't push him to move a relationship forward, he's rushing it forward.

And while you want an ardent man, watch out for love-bomber types. Healthy men come on strong, too, but there's a difference between a healthy guy who pushes things forward in a loving and romantic way and a love-bomber type who unhealthily tries to gain control over you in the beginning and whose actions don't match up over time to his words. That type of man pushes you to fall for him quickly, so it's harder for you to leave and so you're easier to control. When a man is overbearing in the beginning, doesn't respect your boundaries, and gets mean, manipulative, or stalker-ish, he's likely a love-bomber type.

A healthy man respects that you're pacing a relationship (even if he wants to see you more and is slightly annoyed that he can't see you more). When you pace a relationship with a healthy mature man, he doesn't get mean, manipulative, or stalker-ish.

The timeline for how a relationship progresses is different for every couple. Many factors, including whether there are young children involved, whether the couple wants children, and whether the relationship is long-distance, should be considered. But when a woman holds out for courtship, an interested man typically asks for exclusivity around the three-month mark or earlier. Some men never ask, assuming you're exclusive, and then one day they'll pop the question, making the relationship permanent via a proposal. Typically in the latter situation, you'll have a good feeling that this man is serious about you. Within a year, or even slightly less, a man will typically propose, but if he doesn't, you can ask his intentions. It's not fair for a man to waste more than one year of your time. You can't date indefinitely.

Hold Back Even With Mr. Right

When a man comes on strong, some women — instead of pacing a relationship — reciprocate and come on strong in return. It feels so good and they feel so connected to him that they see nothing wrong with rushing things. He's rushing the relationship along, and they want to do the same. However, it's not smart to think with your heart. Think with your head.

Nina, 43, a client who lives outside Paris, suggested to her besotted boyfriend, Finn, 47, that they go to the nursing home where his mother lived so she could meet his mother. The next time Finn visited his mother, he brought Nina along. Finn was enamored with Nina, but she said he was moody after the visit. When you force a man's hand, he gets resentful.

When you give up control and let a man plan, the plan often unfolds better than expected. Other times, a man shows his true colors, but that's good too, because you want to know this sooner rather than later.

Asking A Man's Intentions

Men know soon after they meet you whether they can live without you. While a man does know quickly if you're *the one*, he may drag his feet. This is one time when it's okay to give a guy a push. He may love you but is happy with the way things are. Even a good guy can date indefinitely. Commitment can be scarier for men.

Or if he has baggage and it's the second or third time around or beyond, he may take longer. Or if he's young, he might not feel ready to take the plunge.

Sometimes you can have an intentions talk before one year, depending on your age and specific circumstances. But if one year has gone by and there's no sign of a proposal, you have to say something. It's not fair that a man takes up more than one year of your life without locking you down with an engagement.

There are times after you're engaged that you'll need to wait before you tie the knot. It could take time to merge two households, or there could be other reasons you need to wait for the actual wedding ceremony. But there should be no reason why he can't commit within about one year with an engagement. Men's psyches are into you or not, and if they aren't, you want to know sooner rather than later. Plus, your psyche needs to know within one year where you stand.

If you've been dating someone for more than a year and he still has no idea if you're *the one*, cut your losses. If a man says he loves you and sees a future but isn't ready, you may have to give a strict ultimatum. Depending on his reason for not being ready, you need to nicely and calmly give him a date when you expect a ring or else you're moving on. And you have to move on if he continues to drag his feet.

You can't let a man waste your time. You deserve to be with someone who is sure.

Sometimes men need to lose you or realize how hard it is to live without you before they propose. You may have to disappear for a few weeks for him to realize what he's lost. He may come back with a ring and say something like, "Those two weeks without you were the hardest weeks of my life. I want you in my life." A guy who can't live without you will fight for you and quickly become sure.

A guy who doesn't see or want a future will never see you again or will try to get you to continue to date him without a commitment. This is a great thing—even if you don't see it at the moment—because this means there's a better plan for you. If the ultimatum doesn't work, thank your lucky stars because you saved yourself time. He wasn't your Mr. Right. I've seen guys stay in relationships with women for years and never marry them. The man has excuse after excuse, and the woman waits around because she believes his excuses. Then the couple breaks up, and he's married within a year to someone else.

Consider The Timing Of The Ultimatum

The timeline for when to give "the talk" is different for everyone. A lot depends on your age and goals and the type of baggage coming into the relationship. Also, be sensitive to certain holidays and anniversaries, like the anniversary of the death of a loved one. If the holidays are coming, wait, you don't want to spoil the time — or any surprises he has in store.

Sometimes you already have your answer through a lackluster Valentine's Day, which is what happened to one client, Annalise, 39. Valentine's Day was 10 months into their relationship, and it was awful. Corey, 40, skipped the day of Valentine's Day (no call or even a text), but he did contact her about her regular Saturday night date. She was hoping he had something special planned.

On the date, Corey never mentioned Valentine's Day. He previously mentioned that they would go on a snowboarding trip during Valentine's weekend with some of his friends, although she didn't snowboard. (He loved to snowboard.) On their weekend date, he told her that none of his friends wanted to go away that weekend anyhow, so he never planned anything. She emailed me from the bathroom. "None of his friends wanted to go away this weekend. NO KIDDING!! They know what he doesn't — that Valentine's weekends are for your girlfriend, especially your first Valentine's together. I want to break up with him right now!!!" Instead of breaking up, she asked him where things were going and got a lackluster answer. They broke up.

Luckily, Annalise had been multi-dating and moved on quickly. She's currently dating a loving boyfriend who is already talking marriage, and they've only been dating six months. She's taking this slow, but we think he's *the one*.

Skye, 53, was dating Evan, 55, who told her on the fifth

date he was falling in love with her. Their relationship unfolded like beautiful poetry. He wasn't in a rush to seal the deal with a formal commitment because he'd been through a contentious divorce and explosive custody battle. Skye was compassionate, and didn't want to give an ultimatum at first, but it was not fair for her to stay with him for longer than one year without any formal commitment talk. About one year in, she asked him where the relationship was going, and he bought her a ring soon after. He was afraid to lose her. They've been happily married for five years, and he always tells her, "You changed how I think about marriage. I used to think it was a trap, but that's because I was with the wrong person. Even when we argue, it's good because I'm with you."

The Bottom Line

Never rush a man. You'll find that, most of the time, the man is the one rushing you to move to the next step. However, one of the few times you have to give a man a gentle push is if he doesn't propose within one year. Even a good man may drag his feet when it comes to proposing. You have a right to give a gentle but firm ultimatum after about one year because you can't let a man waste your time if he doesn't have serious intentions.

When you know how men think — they do know within a year, and usually much sooner, whether you're that special someone — you'd never hang on beyond one year (unless perhaps you're very young, not sure yourself, or in an exceptional circumstance).

Dream *Girl* Dialogue

Here's how to ask a man's intentions and how to respond if he suggests living together as an alternative to marriage.

A good script to get the conversation going when you've been dating a man for around a year is, **"I've enjoyed our time together, but I'm wondering where this is going."** Depending on what he says and how he says it, you may have to cut him off until he's ready to commit. But don't wait long for a man to come back to you. Usually when a man has serious intentions, he won't leave you hanging for too long.

Sometimes a man will say he loves you and sees a future but asks, "What's the rush?" Tell him, **"I'm old-fashioned and don't believe in dating longer than a year without a formal commitment."**

When you ask a man's intentions, do it in a calm and concise way. Anything else works against you.

When a guy doesn't see a future, all you need to do is say, **"Okay,"** or **"Okay, no problem,"** as calmly as possible and never see him again. Plan a singles vacation pronto.

Sometimes a man will suggest living together. If a good man whom you're serious about and want to marry asks you to live with him, say, **"I don't believe in living together."**

Some women tell me they want to live with a man before marriage, but this type of an arrangement usually works against a woman's interests. A man gets to sleep with you and have you in his life as a girlfriend, while you may or may not be wasting your time. If you want to get married to this man, it's best to be sure that he has serious intentions before living together. If you're okay with living with a man casually and okay with him possibly moving on to someone else, then by all means live with him. But if you're looking for the brand of relationship I'm writing about, refrain from living with him until you are engaged — or, even better, wait until you're married.

If he presses and asks why you don't believe in it, you can reply, **"I'm just old-fashioned on this topic."** He'll get the message that if he wants to live with you, he'll have to put a ring on it. The ones who can't live without you will do so.

Conclusion

Now you have a great grasp of how a good man in love behaves when he's truly interested in you. You should also understand what modern-day courtship looks like. These strategies make dating so much easier and lead you to Mr. Right much quicker.

No matter what part of the world you're from, these strategies work. Men are the same everywhere. Don't make excuses for a man based on the country he's from. I have clients all over the world. There are great men everywhere who respond to courtship. I've found over and over again — whether it's London, Paris, NYC, small towns, or remote islands — the same situations with men come up. These scripts and weeding-out strategies work the world over.

Sometimes women will complain, "Men in this country won't ask women out." Or, "Men don't want to get married and commit in this country. They prefer to live together." Or, "Men are cheap here. They always want to split the bill." Or, "The men in my city won't ask women out for a second date if they don't get sex on a first date." These women are frustrated that the guy they like isn't courting them. They blame his locale for his bad behavior, and they decide courtship doesn't work in his particular region. This way of thinking is wrong.

After coaching women all over the world for more than 15 years and researching this topic, I've concluded that no matter where a guy is from, if he's a healthy man who is deeply interested in you, he'll respond to the courtship strategies I've outlined throughout the book.

A healthy guy pursues you if he wants to be with you.

Don't make excuses, like Simone, 49, from Norway, who met a cute guy on Tinder. After their first drink and apps date, he asked her to split the bill, so she did. He was her type—a gorgeous, tall, dark, and handsome lawyer who made her laugh. She hadn't been attracted to a guy for so long. She loved the few hours she spent with him. It took her mind off her frustrating retail job selling high-end clothing to snobby women and the difficulties she was having with her teenage son. She convinced herself he wanted to split the bill because, "Men in this country like women who are feminists."

Simone waited for him to text her for a second date, but a week went by and she hadn't heard from him. "I'm going to see how he's doing because men in this country want to be pursued," Simone said. She texted him. He never responded.

Simone isn't the only woman who has made excuses. Who wants to believe that a guy you like isn't into you? But if you're realistic, you'll weed out guys who are bad for you quickly, and you'll find your pearl. A guy who doesn't want to pay—like the man Simone dated—could be a stingy man who would never pay for a woman. Is that the type of man you want? A man who has no idea how to court a woman? Usually, men like that end up treating women as colleagues or platonic friends, and the relationships turn casual.

Yes, some men may be confused about courtship in this day and age, but even these guys—if they're into you—aren't going to risk offending you by asking you to split the bill. Plus, often a guy can tell during your date if you're the type who appreciates courtship. Women who don't respect courtship have masculine tendencies and will take the lead, driving the conversation forward, and they aren't able to receive gestures, like a man filling up their water glass or pulling out their chair. A man senses when he's with a feminine woman. If he senses you're comfortable receiving and if he feels that spark, his protective instincts will kick in and he'll want to treat you to dinner.

The courting process is essential to lay a romantic foundation for your relationship. It's a beautiful memory that you can all talk about 50 years later—something that keeps the bond strong, in times of good and bad.

A man who feels a spark will move your relationship forward. He'll be with you on Saturday nights. He'll integrate you into his inner circle. He'll drive to you or take public transportation to be with you on dates. A man in romantic love will put a ring on it and take you off the market because he wants you in his life. (If you're not looking to get married but still want a serious relationship with a loving man, these strategies will also help with that.) No matter where you live, you can have a beautiful love story with a man. The world is large, and he's out there!

As you go out into the world, armed with these strategies and knowledge, I want to leave you with some reminders.

Love Is The Best Type Of Riches

Growing up, I'd hear older and wiser women say, "Find a man who loves you more than you love him." These were women who'd been through marriages and relationships. They'd been through it all and seen it all. I didn't quite get that phrase back then. At this stage in my life and in my career as a dating and relationship coach, it makes perfect sense.

Courtship is easier when it's with a man who loves you more than you love him. When you truly understand men, you'll realize that because of the imbalance in the way women and men see romantic relationships, it's better if you end up with a man who loves you more. That way the relationship is more even.

You may think, *Well, why can't it be equal? Why can't we both love one another the same amount?* You certainly can, and those relationships can work out. But I've found that when a woman is with a man who loves her a little more, she's more content. This is because most women are more emotional and care more about relationships than men. There's a natural imbalance from the beginning. When you're with a man who loves you more, the relationship ends up being more in sync.

These relationships flow better. You'll have good and bad times in any relationship. It's better to have a loving man who's with you 100 percent, someone who makes love easy.

Be Picky About The Right Things

Many women today are picky about the wrong things

and lax about the qualities that mean the most.

Some women want a man with Brad Pitt's star power, but even Brad Pitt isn't good enough for these women. They want him to be 10 years younger than Pitt and have an MBA from Harvard University. They also want him to be funny, sweet, witty, and a good dresser.

These women are less picky, however, when it comes to the inner game. They don't care if he skips weekends. They cut him slack if he doesn't feel like driving to their area for the date. They make excuses for his "complicated" baggage, and they accept crumbs emotionally. Think hard about your priorities and the type of man you want to spend your life with.

Take The Right Actions

I want to stress that this isn't about being a doormat at all. As you see throughout the book, I advocate standing up for yourself when necessary. I believe you should leave a situation if you're with Mr. Wrong. I also believe you should be aggressive about many things, including learning to understand men and grasping these courtship strategies.

Courtship is not passive. It's about learning to receive from a man and seeing what he's capable of giving you. You keep your eyes open during the courtship process and evaluate his qualities to see if he's someone you can have a future with. Women who respect courtship are the ones who truly understand the differences between men and women.

You work on your inner game, bettering yourself while on your way to meeting your ideal partner.

You work on your outer game, too. Work out. Get blowouts, manicures, pedicures, and wax your eyebrows and everywhere else that needs it. Get lash extensions. Dress for men, and always look your absolute best.

Take massive actions to meet men—online dating, singles-related events, fix-ups, and other ways.

More than 50 percent of my clients have met their husbands online, so definitely try it and stay on it. Many people try for a month and get off, saying, "It's such a waste of time." But it can take longer than one month to meet Mr. Right. Who knows when he's going to show up?

You need to be out and about, in the swim of things online and in real life, to up your chances of meeting your soul mate. If you use my strategies, online dating and dating in real life will be much more efficient.

Don't Give Up

When you're Miss Right and meet Mr. Right, this advice works. But it doesn't mean all men act like princes at the drop of the hat.

A guy could simply be bad news and is looking for low-level relationships. He may not be capable of or interested in a healthy relationship. Some men aren't relationship-minded. They may like some things about being in one—

like sex and having a date to show off at events and parties. Beyond that, they aren't looking for intimacy. Or, a man may not be ready for a serious intimate relationship. He may not be feeling it with you. This can be hard to accept. But all men have types. Your type may not rev up his engine.

Don't lose sleep over any of these guys. Move on. Beautiful ladies, don't waste time on men who don't appreciate you. Hold out for the one who treats you right, who loves and adores you, who treats you like the princess you are. He's out there. Don't forget that!

Remember, if a guy doesn't like you as much as you like him, it's not that you aren't wonderful. Don't waste your precious energy fighting it or crying over it. Don't let this dampen your self-esteem. I want you to have high self-esteem and confidence. Just realize that men have types, and if you're not his type, there's nothing you can do except move on quickly so you find Mr. Right.

Sometimes the dating trenches can be frustrating. You may feel guilty for hurting someone. You may get hurt yourself. The one you like may not like you back. You may have to break up with a great guy who you don't like enough. This can be tough on your emotions. You may feel so exhausted from dating you can't go on one more date.

This is why you'll see the spiritual gym referenced throughout this book. It's important to have something that keeps you going when dating gets tough.

Tell yourself every failure or setback on the way to finding Mr. Right is getting you one step closer to him. Think to

Karenna Alexander

yourself, "I'm one frog closer to meeting my prince."

Sometimes it's easier to look at dating as if it's a numbers game. Realize, if you keep lining up dates, you'll find your Prince Charming eventually.

Always remember: the one you're seeking is looking for you, too!

If you have faith in yourself and the courtship process, keep taking action, and follow the advice in this book, you'll get great results.

About the Author

As a journalist with a master's degree from Columbia University Graduate School of Journalism, I became certified as a dating coach from the authors of *The Rules* and began coaching part-time while I was a full-time reporter, then editor.

I loved coaching so much, I incorporated my new passion into my daily life as a hard-core journalist, writing an advice column on relationships for the print and online publication where I worked. By day, I had the legal beat. By night, I had a "Dear Abby" type column, answering questions from readers about life and love.

Soon my passion for helping others completely took over, and I began coaching as a career, helping women date better, be happier in their relationships, get engaged, and get married.

I also got certified as a matchmaker by the Matchmaking Institute and added matchmaking services on top of dating coaching services, because so many clients had a hard time finding *the one*. I no longer offer matchmaking services because I've been able to help more women into amazing relationships, get them engaged and married through coaching.

Subscribe to my newsletter: karennaalexander.com/contact-us. You will get occasional dating tips through email and notices about special coaching offers.

Website: karennaalexander.com
Facebook: karennaalexanderllc
Twitter: @coachkarenna

I wish you the best out there!

Karenna Alexander

Need More Dating Advice?

This book is a great start, but every woman and every relationship is different. I'd love to talk with you to hear the challenges you're facing and help you make a plan to find Mr. Right. If you're in the trenches of dating and want someone to give you feedback that leads to a happy relationship, I'm here for you.

I offer hourly coaching sessions and bulk packages, as well as personalized courses targeting specific areas, including appearance, taking the right dating actions, mindset, and modern courtship dating strategies.

If you'd like to learn more about my services, fill out this form on my website: karennaalexander.com/contact-us.

Acknowledgments

Many thanks to:

My clients and fans — you are the best.

Aurelia Trgo — my oldest RG friend for her careful reading of this book.

Kay Gimmestad and Peter Bryer — my astute first readers.

Alina — my supersmart sounding board.

Kyle Haines, Michele Cabay, and Tisha Benoit — for being superb listeners.

Editors Kelly Carr and Melissa Wuske — for polishing this book to perfection.

Diane Krause — for being a fount of information.

The men who spoke freely to me during interviews.

My mom, Joan, and my dad, Ned — who gave me more than they will ever know.

Scott — for a quiet place to write and a new printer, etc.

Brad — for giving freely of his counsel.

The irreplaceable Ellen Fein and Sherrie Schneider — who started the magic.

Made in the USA
Las Vegas, NV
28 April 2023

71216546R00154